Effective Teacher Induction & Mentoring
ASSESSING THE EVIDENCE

Effective Teacher Induction & Mentoring

ASSESSING THE EVIDENCE

Michael Strong

Foreword by Richard Ingersoll

TEACHERS
COLLEGE
PRESS

Teachers College, Columbia University
New York and London

Published by Teachers College Press, 1234 Amsterdam Avenue, New York, NY 10027

Figure 4.1 is reprinted from *Trends in Cognitive Sciences 4*(4), D.J. Simons, "Attentional Capture and Inattentional Blindness," pp. 147–155, copyright 2000, with permission from Elsevier.

Figures 4.7 and 4.8 are reprinted from G.A. Fischer (1967), "Measuring Ambiguity,"*American Journal of Psychology 80*(4), pp. 543, 545. From *American Journal of Psychology*. Copyright 1967 by the Board of Trustees of the University of Illinois. Used with permission of the author and the University of Illinois Press.

Library of Congress Cataloging-in-Publication Data

Strong, Michael, 1945–
  Effective teacher induction and mentoring: assessing the evidence / Michael Strong.
  p. cm.
  Includes bibliographical references and index.
  ISBN 978-0-8077-4933-3 (pbk.) —ISBN 978-0-8077-4934-0 (hardcover)
    1. Teacher orientation—United States. 2. Mentoring in education—United States. 3. Teacher effectiveness—United States, I. Title.
LB1729.S77 2008
371.10973—dc22   2008032908

ISBN: 978-0-8077-4933-3 (paper)
ISBN: 978-0-8077-4934-0 (hardcover)

Printed on acid-free paper
Manufactured in the United States of America
16 15 14 13 12 11 10 09   8 7 6 5 4 3 2 1

To my family, Jeanie and Sam Strong,
and in memory of my mother, Liz.

Contents

Foreword

As a high school teacher in the 1980s, I never encountered induction or mentoring. Indeed, I am not sure I would have known what those terms meant. Support, guidance and orientation programs were largely nonexistent in the schools in which I taught. And, as I learned in my subsequent career as an educational researcher, my experience was not unique.

Educational historians have long told us that the teaching occupation has not had the kind of structured induction and initiation processes common to many white-collar occupations and characteristic of the traditional professions. Although elementary and secondary teaching involves intensive interaction with youngsters, the work of teachers, ironically, is largely done in isolation from colleagues. This can be especially difficult for new entrants, who upon accepting a teaching position in a school, are often left on their own to succeed or fail within the confines of their own classrooms—an experience likened to being lost at sea. Indeed, critics have long assailed teaching as an occupation that cannibalizes its young and in which the initiation of new teachers is akin to a "sink or swim," "trial by fire," or "boot camp" experience.

Perhaps not surprisingly, teaching has also traditionally been characterized as an occupation with high levels of attrition, especially among beginners. All occupations, of course, experience some loss of new entrants—either voluntarily because newcomers decide to not remain, or involuntarily because employers deem them to be unsuitable. In teaching, however, newcomers have long had far higher rates of attrition than in other professions.

In my own research I have also discovered a strong link between the perennially high rates of beginning teacher attrition and the shortages that seem to perennially plague teaching. The data show that our school systems' widely publicized staffing problems are not solely, or even primarily, due to teacher shortages, that is, in the conventional sense that too few teachers are being produced and recruited. In contrast, the data indicate that school staffing problems are to a significant extent a result of a revolving door, where large numbers of teachers depart teaching long before retirement.

Fortunately, the sink-or-swim model has increasingly become a thing of the past. Over the past decade, a growing number of states and school districts have developed and implemented induction programs designed to provide support, guidance, and orientation for new teachers. Typically these programs are meant to serve as a "bridge" from student of teaching to teacher of students. But, like the induction processes common to other occupations, there are a number of different, and sometimes conflicting, purposes behind teacher induction programs. Among them are support, socialization, adjustment, development, and assessment. Moreover, teacher induction can refer to a variety of different types of activities—classes, workshops, orientations, seminars, and especially, mentoring. The latter, in turn, also come in a wide variety of forms. Mentoring programs, for instance, can vary from a single meeting between mentor and mentee at the beginning of a school year, to a highly structured program involving frequent meetings over a couple of years between mentors and mentees who are provided with release time from their normal teaching schedules.

All of this poses difficulties for those engaged in the very important, but very practical, matter of deciding which, if any program, activity, mechanism to employ in schools. To be sure, there has been a growth in research on the variety and effects of a wide array of these initiatives. However, the research itself also greatly varies in focus, rigor, method, applicability, and conclusion. Hence, there is a need for a careful sifting, assessment and summary of what the research tells us. What do we know, what do we not know, and what do we need to know about teacher induction? Can we definitively say that existing teacher induction programs help teachers? Do we know which components, types, and designs are more—or less—effective? Do we have any evidence on whether such programs are worth their cost? Do different kinds of schools and teachers require different kinds of induction programs?

Michael Strong clearly, carefully and thoroughly examines the research to see what answers it provides. This volume is a unique and valuable resource for researchers, policy makers, school leaders, and education practitioners interested in helping new teachers survive and succeed in our schools.

—*Richard Ingersoll*

Preface

The idea of having a mentor is appealing to most people. A person who is dedicated to helping one learn and succeed is a luxury most of us do not get to enjoy during our lifetime. Mentoring has, however, become increasingly commonplace as one among several approaches to assisting new teachers as they develop their practice during the earliest years of their careers. Few novice teachers are likely to pass up the opportunity to work with a mentor, while they may view workshops and seminars with a little less enthusiasm. It is a costly undertaking to organize mentoring for all the new teachers in a school district, especially large urban districts with high rates of turnover, and a body of research is slowly developing to examine how it is done and whether it is effective. This book lays out the findings from much of this research, some of which I have conducted myself during the last 10 years in my position as Director of Research at the New Teacher Center at the University of California, Santa Cruz. I offer my opinion on this research and its findings, on methodology, and on problems and issues that researchers may or may not have considered. I also review what needs to happen for educators to be in possession of enough facts to determine whether mentoring and induction programs are effective, and if they are a sound investment for the future of teaching. In short, as the subtitle of this book suggests, I assess the evidence.

As a researcher, I am persuaded by empirical evidence over promises, conjecture, and opinion. I advocate that educational decision makers be the same way. All too often legislators and administrators make decisions about schools and teaching without any research to back them up. Research takes time and money, knowledge and expertise, and collaboration and partnerships among schools and universities. Even when the research happens, its findings may come too late, or lack dissemination among the people who most need to learn of them. It is my hope that the information in this book will be of use to those who are in the business of making decisions about new teachers, those who are learning about teaching and educational research, and those who work with new teachers and teachers in training.

I am grateful to Ellen Moir, Executive Director of the New Teacher Center, for hiring me as Director of Research when I was new to the field of teacher induction, and to my fellow researchers Betty Achinstein, Adele Hermann, Stephen Fletcher, Casia Freitas, Anthony Kuan, Lisa Johnson, Linda St. John, and Anthony Villar for their support in all aspects of my work with them and for all their own great work. I am grateful, too, for the collaboration of other educational researchers, notably Sharon Feiman-Nemser, Richard Ingersoll, Sandra Odell, Stephen Ross, Allan Sterbinsky, and Jian Wang, all of whom have been my mentors to some degree. Thanks, also, to Dan Fallon and the Carnegie Corporation for supporting my research with funds as well as encouragement.

Chapter 1

Setting the Scene

On Tuesday, January 7, 2003, an article appeared in England's *Guardian* newspaper about Kesner Ridge, a 24-year-old who was considering quitting teaching midway through her second year.[1] What made the story newsworthy was the fact that she had won an award the previous year for most outstanding new teacher. She said she felt overwhelmed with new government initiatives and the huge workload, and disillusioned "because you never have time to finish anything and do it properly." This story accompanied the publication of a national survey commissioned by the General Teaching Council in the United Kingdom that revealed one in three new teachers expect to quit during their first five years.

Similar statistics have been reported in the United States. The National Commission on Teaching and America's Future (NCTAF)[2] estimated that 1,000 teachers quit the profession each working day, and another 1,000 retire. Furthermore, according to NCTAF, three teachers leave poor schools for every two that move from wealthier schools.

SUPPORT FOR NEW TEACHERS

One strategy adopted by school districts in order to reverse teacher attrition has been to provide teachers with some extra assistance during the induction phase (usually defined as the first one to three years of a teacher's career).

New teacher support typically starts before the academic year begins with a day or two of orientation to the school and district. Once they start work in their classrooms, teachers may receive extra forms of assistance from among a variety of options. Sometimes, for example, they are assigned a mentor; or they may have a reduced teaching load in order to attend professional development sessions or observe veteran teachers; and they might be part of a professional network or receive other extra resources, depending on district policies and budgets.

1

By the 1990s, 56.4% of teachers with up to 3 years experience indicated they participated in an induction program.[3] Now, with the twenty-first century well on its way, induction and mentoring for beginning teachers have increased in popularity in the United States to the extent that, as of 2008, induction was mandated and funded in 17 states. Leading this effort was California, with its Beginning Teacher Support and Assessment (BTSA) program, funded through a teacher credentialing block grant. The exact nature of this support is determined by individual districts, but it usually involves the services of a mentor.

Induction and mentoring programs for new teachers, then, may take a variety of forms, including some or all of the components mentioned earlier. In their analysis of data from the 1999–2000 Schools and Staffing Survey (SASS)[4] that polls a stratified national sample of some 50,000 teachers, and its supplement, the Teacher Follow-up Survey (TFS), Tom Smith and Richard Ingersoll reviewed the distribution among new teachers of induction program features referenced in the survey.[5] These features included assignment to a mentor from the same or different area of teaching, reduced teaching load or number of preparations, collaborative planning time with other teachers, extra classroom assistance in the form of a teacher aide, and developmental seminars. Of course there are other possible characteristics of induction programs and variations on these components. For example, mentors may receive release time from teaching in order to support beginning teachers, or they may have to do this work in addition to a full teaching load. Mentors may or may not receive training and compensation for their extra activities. Beginning teachers may have the opportunity to observe veteran teachers, may be teamed with an experienced teacher, or may be given preferable assignments. These program nuances are not measured in the SASS.

Smith and Ingersoll analyzed the teachers' responses on the SASS, computed how many received each of the features of induction programs, and characterized four levels of induction: 3% had no induction; 56% received basic induction (some kind of mentor and supportive communication with school or department administration); 26% received basic induction plus collaboration (mentors from teachers in their own fields, regular or supportive communication with administration, common planning time or regularly scheduled collaboration with other teachers in their subject area, and participation in a seminar for beginning teachers); and fewer than 1% of the teachers reported receiving the full set of supports, described as basic induction plus collaboration plus teacher network plus extra resources package (the four previous components plus participation in an external network of teachers, a reduced number of preparations, and assignment of a teacher's aide).

I look more closely at Smith and Ingersoll's study in Chapter 3. For now, it serves to introduce the variety of forms that induction programs can take. Their analysis simplifies the possible combinations of features that any particular program may have, however, in that they clump together components in order to conduct their regression analyses, and because they are forced to consider only those features explored by the SASS.

IMPLORING TEACHER QUALITY

Sharon Feiman-Nemser and her colleagues urge us to think "beyond support" when considering the induction of beginning teachers.[6] They make the point that, while giving new teachers some kind of help is better than leaving them to sink or swim, emotional or psychological assistance alone is not enough. Induction programs, they argue, should include elements not only of support, but also the development and assessment of teaching skills.

The passing of the No Child Left Behind Act (NCLB) of 2001 (Public Law No. 107-110) had some implications for new teachers. While the act discusses *teacher quality*, it makes no mention of induction support. NCLB requires that, in order for states to receive federal funding, all teachers must, by the end of the 2006–07 school year, be "highly qualified," as defined in the law. A highly qualified teacher is one who has (1) fulfilled the state's certification and licensing requirements, (2) obtained at least a bachelor's degree, and (3) demonstrated subject-matter expertise.[7]

NCLB defines teacher quality as a concept comprising such characteristics as teacher demographics, aptitude, professional preparation, college majors, SAT and teacher examination scores, teacher licensure and certification, and prior professional work experiences. With increasing recognition of the importance of mentoring as the preferred means of induction support for beginning teachers, it is reasonable to suggest, that, if supported by the evidence, mentoring should be built into the notion of teacher quality. Mentoring is also a bridge to *teacher effectiveness*, a concept that describes the quality of teachers in terms of the outcomes of their teaching, namely student learning and achievement, student engagement in the learning process, and the context of their teaching, sometimes described as the culture of the school. Mentors, then, have the potential to affect both teacher quality and teacher effectiveness. We need empirical evidence, however, to determine whether this potential is realized. The proliferation of induction and mentoring programs to support beginning teachers has generated a need to understand in what ways the programs influence various teacher outcomes beyond mere satisfaction with the program. These include decisions to stay in teaching (retention), teaching practice (teacher development), and possible effects on student learning (student academic achievement). The review of research that forms the central focus of this book will assist us in making this determination.

Chapter 2

A History of Mentoring and Induction for Teachers

The word *mentor* has its origin in the name of a character in Greek literature: When Odysseus departed for the Trojan War he left his son Telemachus under the charge of his friend Mentor. Its use as a term referring generally to a trusted friend, counselor, or teacher can be traced back to the 1699 book *Les Aventures de Télémaque* (*The Adventures of Telemachus*) by the French author François Fénelon. The mentor relationship required that the mentor provide copious amounts of wisdom, learning, and dedication, while the protégé, or mentee, was expected to honor the mentor's greater experience, knowledge, and seniority. Each party respects the other, in spite of the asymmetrical relationship.

In its application to professional settings over the years, the principles of mentoring have shown up under different guises, and have become somewhat narrower. During the Middle Ages skilled craftsmen hired young people as apprentices for minimal wages and an opportunity to receive formal training in their chosen craft. Today there are paid internships in professions such as mental health, law, engineering, and accounting, as well as unpaid internships for students of different levels from high school to university graduates. In all of these settings the participants have the characteristics of mentors and protégés, with the formal goal of providing the learner with essential skills that are best imparted by an experienced professional. Formal mentoring programs involve assignment of a mentor, training, official program goals, and some kind of assessment or evaluation. In addition, informal mentoring relationships sometimes develop between two employees, where similar outcomes may result for the learner.

Past research in organizations has demonstrated the positive outcomes of mentoring. Corporate presidents have reported having mentors who were vital to their success.[1] In one study nearly two thirds of the prominent executives reviewed had mentors, and the mentored group received higher salaries, bonuses, and total compensation than did executives in the nonmentored group.[2] A recent meta-analysis of such research by Tammy Allen from the University of South Florida and her colleagues indicated that former protégés tend to be paid more, promoted more often, and are more positive about their careers than those who have never been mentored.[3]

Kathy Kram studied mentor–protégé dyads and identified two types of mentor functions.[4] The first is career-specific support that enhances advancement in the organization, and includes mentoring functions such as providing sponsorship, encouraging exposure and visibility, coaching, protection, and giving challenging assignments. The second type of support is psychosocial. This relates to the more interpersonal aspects of the relationship that enhance self-confidence, self-identity, and feelings of effectiveness. These are achieved through the mentor's provision of role modeling, accepting behavior, counseling, and friendship. Subsequent work by various researchers has found empirical support for Kram's broad mentor functions.[5]

Formal mentoring programs blossomed during the 1980s. Michael Zey developed a Mutual Benefits model of mentoring programs drawn from social exchange theory, which was based on the belief that people enter into and remain part of relationships in order to meet certain needs. Participants may outgrow these needs or they may continue to benefit indefinitely. Social exchange theory assumes no determined termination point. What Zey added to this model was the notion that the organization (such as a school, corporation, or government agency) that contains the mentor and protégé also benefits from the interaction.[6] This implies that researchers should measure outcomes beyond those that accrue only to the mentor or mentee. In the case of teachers, for example, this might include the school, the district, or the students.

The term *induction* refers to the initial stage or phase of one's career, or to the system of support that may be provided during that phase. *Mentoring,* a term often used synonymously with the term *induction,* refers only to one aspect of an induction support program, and is thus subsumed in the notion of induction rather than synonymous with it.

THE GROWTH OF INDUCTION PROGRAMS FOR TEACHERS

The school reform movement of the 1980s saw the introduction of beginning teacher programs developed by local school districts, university education departments, and state agencies.[7] These induction programs were designed to have mentor teachers assist and support novice teachers in their professional development.[8] Key goals of the programs were to retain new teachers in the profession and help those teachers advance through the three developmental stages described by David Berliner: competent, proficient, and expert.[9] Beginning teacher programs were variously instigated at the local and state level (school districts, county offices of education, state departments of education, institutions of higher education), but the major policy initiative for their creation occurred at the state level.

Carol Furtwengler conducted a thorough review of state policies and provisions for beginning teachers during the "reform" era of the 1980s.[10] She reported that, prior to 1984, only 8 states had initiated policy for beginning teacher programs. An additional 26 states started programs during the years 1984 through 1992. Of these 34 states, 18 mandated statewide programs (Connecticut, Florida, Georgia, Indiana, Kentucky, Maine, Mississippi, New Jersey, New Mexico, North Carolina, Ohio, Oklahoma, Pennsylvania, South Dakota, Tennessee, Utah, Virginia, and West Virginia). Tennessee received no funding to implement its program; Georgia, South Dakota, and Virginia implemented and later rescinded their statewide mandated programs.

The 16 states that did not mandate statewide programs either implemented pilot programs or provided competitive grant money to local school districts for beginning teacher programs (Alabama, California, Delaware, Idaho, Kansas, Louisiana, Minnesota, Missouri, Montana, New Hampshire, New York, Oregon, Texas, Washington, West Virginia, and Wisconsin). Kansas, Missouri, and Wisconsin discontinued fiscal support for their pilot programs. Meanwhile, Virginia and Georgia replaced their rescinded statewide programs with competitive grant money for local pilot programs.

In recent years the *"Quality Counts"* issues of *Education Week* publish an annual review of the U.S. education scene, including an updated survey of state mandates and provisions for new-teacher programs. This review is not perfectly accurate, and it includes no details on program content, only if a so-called induction program is authorized by each state. The map in Figure 2.1 shows which states had an official new-teacher induction program and which mandated and funded such programs, according to "Quality Counts" as of 2005.

The "Quality Counts" report of 2005 reveals that 30 states mandated new-teacher induction and mentoring, and 16 also provided some funding. This shows considerable growth from their 1998 report, which found that only 14 states mandated new-teacher induction and mentoring. Of course, there is substantial variation among the programs outlined by the states, and then further variation among the programs as they are implemented in the schools. Among the 30 states mandating new-teacher induction in 2006, only five provided a

Figure 2.1. Distribution of Induction Programs by State, 2005.

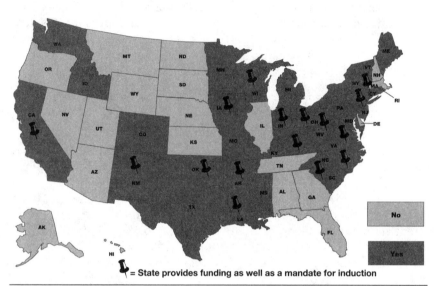

= State provides funding as well as a mandate for induction

Source: NCTAF, 2005. Figure based on data from "Quality counts 2005: No small change"
[Special issue], January 6, 2005, *Education Week, 24*(17), p. 94.

minimum of 2 years of state financed mentoring. The 2008 version of
"Quality Counts,"[11] reports that 22 states fund induction programs for
all new teachers, 25 have mentoring programs for all new teachers, 20
have standards for training mentors, and 2 have reduced workload for
all first-year teachers. These numbers are depicted in Figure 2.2.

Another source of information about the nation's induction and
mentoring programs is the national Schools and Staffing Survey (SASS).
In their analysis of these data, Smith and Ingersoll[12] discovered that
teacher-reported participation in induction programs increased during
the decade from 1990 to 2000. In the 1990–91 school year, about 40% of
beginning teachers said that they had "participated in a formal teacher
induction program, that is, a program to help beginning teachers by assigning them to master or mentor teachers." By 1993–94, the number
increased to just over half of the beginning teachers. By the 1999–2000
school year, participation rates in induction programs rose to about
80%. These numbers suggest that teacher induction programs may be
more numerous than the "Quality Counts" state overview indicates.
In other words, some school districts around the country implement
programs for their beginning teachers, whether or not the state mandates and/or funds them.

Figure 2.2. Number of States with Various New-Teacher Supports, 2007–08

Supports for beginning teachers	States
Induction program for all new teachers funded by state	22
Mentoring program for all new teachers funded by state	25
Mentoring program standards for selecting, training, and/or matching mentors	20
Reduced workload for all first-year teachers	2

FEATURES OF MAJOR INDUCTION PROGRAMS

Having determined that induction and mentoring programs for beginning teachers are now widespread across the United States (and in several other countries also), [13] I now examine the components of several of the most well-developed models.

One of the most widely recognized models for new-teacher support programs was developed by members of the New Teacher Center (NTC) at the University of California, Santa Cruz, where I work. The program has six goals:

- To develop teacher capacity as defined in the *California Standards for the Teaching Profession*
- To direct support toward improving student achievement
- To use formative assessment practices to guide support
- To document professional growth over time
- To model and encourage ongoing self-assessment and reflection
- To foster collaboration and leadership among teachers[14]

In the NTC's comprehensive induction program (situated within California's state program described below), teachers receive the services of a full-time mentor, who has a caseload of no more than 15 new teachers, each of whom is visited at least once a week. New teachers stay in the program for 2 years. Mentors are carefully selected from among an applicant pool of veteran teachers, and matched as closely as possible to mentees according to grade level and subject matter. Mentors typically work for 3 years before returning to their classrooms. They attend an initial 5-day mentor academy to learn about coaching, mentoring, and the use of formative assessment tools. Then throughout their assignment as mentors they meet weekly for half-day training sessions, where they discuss ongoing issues, look at case studies, and generally solve problems. Mentors observe each beginning teacher's classroom at least one hour a week, after which they debrief with the teacher. Early in the year mentors and teachers set goals based on the California teaching standards. Mentors use a formative assessment system developed by the New Teacher Center, which is approved by the state and used by over a hundred districts. The program costs a little over $6,000 per teacher, per year, most of which is funded by the state and the balance by the school district.

The NTC induction program is one of about 150 programs in California that exist within its state-mandated and state-funded Beginning Teacher Support and Assessment (BTSA) program. BTSA began as a pilot in 1992–93 with 15 local programs (collaborations of districts, county offices of education, and universities), supporting 1,100 first- and second-year teachers at a cost of about $5 million. BTSA was expanded in 1997, and in 1998 California enacted legislation requiring an induction program for all beginning teachers. As of 2004–05, 148 BTSA programs were in place, serving 96% of all school districts. State funding for 2005–06 was estimated at $3,675 per teacher for first-year teachers and $3,357 per teacher for second-year teachers, with districts providing an additional $2,000 per teacher in "in-kind" resources (e.g., support from experienced teachers).

There are seven objectives of the BTSA program:

- To provide an effective transition into the teaching career for first- and second-year teachers in California
- To improve the educational performance of students through improved training, information, and assistance for participating teachers
- To enable beginning teachers to be effective in teaching students who are culturally, linguistically, and academically diverse
- To ensure the professional success and retention of new teachers
- To ensure that a support provider provides intensive individualized support and assistance to each participating beginning teacher
- To ensure that an individual induction plan is in place for each participating beginning teacher and is based on an ongoing assessment of the development of the beginning teacher
- To ensure continuous program improvement through ongoing research, development, and evaluation[15]

BTSA programs must meet California's standards of quality and effectiveness for professional teacher induction programs,[16] and must serve teachers for 2 years. Teachers' participation is required in order for them to obtain their clear teaching credential. BTSA is run by the state via a series of regional "clusters" that are coordinated with schools and districts. All programs have some form of mentoring, either fully or partially releasing mentors from teaching or giving full-time teachers an additional stipend and a few release days each year to work with one or two teachers. Mentors may be variously trained in the kinds of coaching their districts espouse and in their formative assessment systems.

The developers of BTSA also created a formative assessment system to be used alongside the BTSA program. Until 2008 they used the California Formative Assessment and Support System for Teachers (CFASST). In 2003 all but 9 of 142 BTSA programs in the state employed CFASST as a central component. In its final form, BTSA/CFASST engaged first- and second-year teachers in a series of 12 "events" (six in each year) based on the California Standards for the Teaching Profession (CSTP).[17] Previous forms of BTSA/CFASST, covering essentially the same topics in very similar ways, were organized with 10 events in Year 1 and 7 events in Year 2. With the guidance of an experienced teacher who has received training as a mentor (known as a support provider), beginning teachers were expected to work through the CFASST events by gathering information about best practices, planning lessons, and receiving feedback on their teaching through observations by the mentor. Beginning teachers were also required to reflect on their practice and develop ways of applying what they have learned to future lessons. This was facilitated by ongoing formative assessment in which the beginning teacher and mentor assess the teaching practice of the beginning teacher and set goals for professional growth, using a formative assessment tool based on the CSTP, called the Descriptions of Practice (DOP).

In 2006 the governor of California signed SB (Senate Bill) 1209, which charged the California Department of Education (CDE) and the California Commission on Teacher Credentialing (CCTC) to revise the formative assessment system for BTSA. In response to this, BTSA put together a design team and developed a new formative assessment system called FACT that began field testing in 2007 and was implemented in 2008. The goal of the new assessment system was "to eliminate duplicative requirements of teacher preparation programs and to maximize candidates' application of knowledge and skills of the *California Standards for the Teaching Profession.*"[18]

Outside California, perhaps the best known induction program is Connecticut's Beginning Educator Support and Training (BEST). The

BEST program grew out of the Education Enhancement Act (EEA) of 1986 and companion legislation, which were the culmination of attempts by two commissioners of education, Mark Shedd and Gerald Tirozzi, to raise teacher licensure standards and make school spending more equitable.

The purposes of the BEST program are fourfold:

- To ensure that beginning teachers have opportunities to strengthen their knowledge of subject matter and instructional strategies, as well as to enhance their understanding of students as learners
- To prepare beginning teachers to successfully develop and demonstrate foundational skills and competencies as well as discipline-specific teaching standards as defined by Connecticut's Common Core of Teaching
- To assist beginning teachers in understanding the school and district's curricular goals and standards, as well as the state standards for student achievement, as defined by Connecticut's Common Core of Learning, Connecticut Framework: K–12 Curricular Goals and Standards, and both the Connecticut Mastery Test (CMT) and Connecticut Academic Performance Test (CAPT)
- To provide the foundation for a process of lifelong learning and professional growth

Ultimately, the goal of BEST program support is to help beginning teachers improve the effectiveness of their instruction, thereby leading to improved student learning.[19]

A crucial component of the BEST program is the teaching portfolio, which documents the relationship between teaching behaviors and student learning within a unit of instruction. Teachers work with a mentor or support team on a regular basis during their first year. Mentors are required to participate in 24 hours of professional development related to new teacher development, the state's teaching standards, and the BEST portfolio assessment process. They receive continuing education credits for mentoring and may or may not earn a stipend. They continue teaching full-time themselves, but receive some release time during which they are expected to provide instructional support to novices and help them reflect on their practice. At least one support team member must be a trained BEST mentor, and at least one should have teaching experience in the appropriate content area.

In addition to mentoring, Connecticut offers subject-specific seminars to beginning teachers that are designed to familiarize them with the state's teaching standards and the portfolio requirements. In their second year with the BEST program, new teachers in most content areas must complete a content-specific portfolio designed to assess their pedagogical knowledge and skills. Each portfolio should include (integrated around a unit) a description of their teaching context, a set of lesson plans, two videotapes of instruction during the unit, samples of student work, and teacher commentaries on their planning, instruction, and assessment of student progress. For those teachers whose performance on the portfolio is judged to be unsatisfactory, they have the opportunity to go through the portfolio process again during their third year of teaching. If their performance on the portfolio remains unsatisfactory, they are ineligible for licensure and are not able to continue teaching in Connecticut.

While the state influences beginning teachers' induction experiences by training mentors, offering subject-specific seminars, and requiring second-year teachers to go through the high-stakes portfolio process, new teachers' experiences are also shaped by district policy related to induction. Some districts supplement the BEST program with a comprehensive array of support activities, thereby potentially fostering high levels of instructional quality. The state contributes $700–$800 per beginning teacher, and districts add a further $1,000–$3,000. All teachers with an initial educator certificate may participate; between 50 to 60% actually do.[20]

Recently the local unions have started a movement to make changes to the BEST program because some teachers are complaining that the portfolio process and other logistical requirements have become too burdensome and evaluative. At the time of writing there have been legislative hearings on this matter, where the Connecticut Education Association is urging changes toward a more comprehensive mentoring model, based on that developed by the NTC.

In contrast to programs based on a nonevaluative mentoring model are those adhering to the concept of Peer Assistance and Review (PAR). PAR started in Toledo, Ohio, in 1981, through the instigation of Dal Lawrence, maverick union president of Toledo's American Federation of Teachers (AFT) affiliate. Drawing from the medical model where doctors mentor interns, Lawrence felt that teacher professionalism could be improved by having expert teachers mentor new teachers. The Toledo Plan was born, whereby a nine-member advisory board (consisting of five teachers and four administrators) would make decisions on assisting and, if necessary, firing new and veteran teachers. For a union man to push the idea of terminating underperforming teachers was controversial, to say the least.

Nevertheless, over the next two decades, a few other districts (notably Cincinnati and Columbus in Ohio; Poway and Mt. Diablo in California; Rochester in New York; Dade County in Florida; and Salt Lake City in Utah) initiated programs modeled on the Toledo Plan of peer review. Typically, PAR programs involve "consulting teachers," (CTs), who are identified for excellence and released from full-time teaching duties for 2 to 3 years, in order to provide mentoring to teachers new to the district or the profession as well as to intervene on behalf of veteran teachers experiencing difficulty. The big difference between this model and other teacher mentoring programs is that CTs, in addition to principals, also conduct the formal personnel evaluations of the "participating teachers" (PTs). CTs report to the districtwide advisory board (called the "PAR panel"). The panel holds hearings several times a year, at which CTs provide reports about PT progress. At the spring hearing or sometimes sooner, the CTs make recommendations about the continued employment of each PT. A PT must meet specified quality standards within a set period of time, usually one year, or face removal from the classroom, as determined by the panel based on the recommendation of the CT, sometimes in concert with the principal. The panel's employment recommendation is passed to the superintendent, who makes a recommendation to the school board, the ultimate arbiter of personnel decisions.

The Toledo Plan is the longest standing example of a PAR program. PTs receive a one-week orientation, after which CTs, with a caseload of 10–12, spend about 20 hours per semester with each PT. Mentor training consists of a 3-day workshop during the summer before CTs start their new role. They are paid to be full-time mentors and stand to gain professional development and enhanced career opportunities. CTs conduct one formal evaluation during each of the two semesters their PTs are in the program. At the end of the year, the advisory board (a PAR panel consisting of union, district, and school representatives) votes to accept or reject the CT's recommendation whether or not the teacher should be rehired. The program costs about $3,500 per beginning teacher.

The PAR model is different from other approaches to induction support in that its focus is as much about teacher evaluation as it is about teacher mentoring. The very notion that a mentor should also be responsible for high-stakes evaluation of teachers is contrary to one of the fundamental tenets of a traditional mentoring program, whose philosophy stresses the importance of keeping evaluation separate from formative assessment. In a program such as that of the New Teacher Center, founded on the principles of cognitive coaching[21] much emphasis is placed on the development of trust between mentor and mentee, with the implication being that trust may be compromised when the mentor is also an evaluator. The PAR line of thinking is that, if anyone is going to be evaluating a beginning teacher, it should be the mentor, who knows the teacher's work better than a principal or other evaluator whose knowledge of the teacher's skills is probably derived from a handful of brief visits to the classroom over the year. An added feature of the PAR model, it may be argued, is that it changes the traditional educational hierarchy, wresting the responsibility for evaluation away from the administration and handing it to the teachers, thereby giving them authority and responsibility for the quality of practice.[22]

The question of whether new teacher evaluation is better performed by the mentor or the principal is open to empirical examination, but a definitive assessment of this issue has yet to be conducted. Brian Yusko and Sharon Feiman-Nemser, after studying two mentoring programs, suggest that assessment and assistance can coexist.[23] Jennifer Goldstein studied the case of one PAR program over 3 years in a California urban school district and reached the following conclusions:

1. PAR teachers were able to spend more time on teacher evaluation than principals.
2. PAR, by linking summative with formative assessment, provided a less arbitrary and more individualized evaluation rooted in standards than typically provided by principals.
3. PAR assessments are more transparent than traditional evaluations.
4. Unions are part of the process, instead of only being involved when a teacher wishes to contest a principal's decision.
5. PAR assessments result in more confidently made evaluations. 6. The level of accountability is higher—12.5% of beginning teachers were "non-renewed" under the PAR system compared to all teachers being found competent under the old process.[24]

Goldstein's findings are all fairly predictable, and because of the case-study design, they do not allow for a clear comparison between PAR and traditional mentoring in order to test the effects of merging the roles of mentor and evaluator. Her findings point us to a conclusion that PAR is an efficient and effective means for evaluating new and experienced teachers, but say little about the quality of the mentoring support the beginning teachers receive under that model. Indeed, her focus was primarily on the CTs rather than the PTs,[25] so we have little insight into the new teachers' perceptions of the quality and nature of their mentoring, or the level of trust they developed toward their mentors.

INDUCTION PROGRAMS IN OTHER COUNTRIES

Induction programs for beginning teachers exist in many countries of the world. They vary in nature and intensity, and they operate in widely different educational environments. Most involve some form of mentoring or coaching, and the focus is on imporving teaching skills.

Several reviews have been made of induction programs in other countries. Two studies examined induction in China, France, Japan, Switzerland, and New Zealand.[26] Another report reviewed programs in 10 Pacific Rim Countries (USA, Canada, Australia, Brunei, Japan, Chinese Taipei, Singapore, Papua New Guinea, Korea, and New Zealand).[27] Further references are made throughout the literature to induction elsewhere, for example in England,[28] Estonia,[29] Germany, France, and Portugal,[30] the Netherlands,[31] and Israel.[32]

Without going into detail about programs in each of the countries mentioned, I list here a few of their salient features. Generally, the main goal of induction programs in other countries is to improve teaching skills. Outside the United States, where a stated goal of programs often is to improve teacher retention, teacher attrition seems to be less of a problem and hence is not a relevant issue. One can speculate on why that may be. In some countries, such as Japan, Germany, and France, teaching is seen as a high-status profession, and to be a new-teacher coach or guide in Japan or China is a highly honored position.[33] Secondary school teaching in France is a very competitive profession, with a probationary phase during which teachers (called *stagiaires*) work part-time with multiple guiding teachers and advisors. Teachers in Switzerland are well paid, and competition is fierce for the few available positions. Many opt for part-time positions in order to get a foot in the door.[34]

Across most countries certain conditions appear to be critical to the perceived success of induction programs: a culture of shared responsibility and support; interaction of new and experienced teachers; a continuum of professional development; down-played assessment; clearly defined goals; and adequate political, financial, and time commitments by relevant authorities. In spite of these common themes, the organization and features of the various teacher induction programs evident in the different countries range widely in scope and duration, as they do within the United States. At one end of the continuum are brief school-level orientations at the beginning of the school year. At the other extreme are multiyear programs that include ongoing orientation, networking, mentoring, and in-service workshops, tailored to the particular needs of teachers in a given context. The organizing authority may be the national government (as in Japan, Papua New Guinea, and Chinese Taipei), the state or territory (as in Australia, Canada, and Korea, or the school or school district (as in Brunei, New Zealand, and Singapore.) [35]

STUDIES OF HOW MENTORS WORK WITH BEGINNING TEACHERS

The nature of mentors' work with beginning teachers will depend both on the specific, practical needs of the new teachers as they encounter the challenges of their first months in the classroom, and on the philosophical approach and goals of the induction program. When the focus is on "reform-minded teaching," mentors will help new teachers develop the relevant dispositions, knowledge, and skills necessary for this kind of work, in addition to carrying out the everyday process of teaching.[36] Sharon Feiman-Nemser uses the term *educative mentoring* to distinguish a more reform-minded approach to mentoring from conventional approaches that emphasize adjusting to the prevailing context, providing technical advice, and giving emotional support. She explains her concept of educative mentoring as follows:

> Educative mentoring rests on an explicit vision of good teaching and an understanding of teacher learning. Mentors who share this orientation attend to beginning teachers' present concerns, questions, and purposes without losing sight of long-term goals for teacher development. They interact with novices in ways that foster an inquiring stance. They cultivate skills and habits that enable novices to learn in and from their practice. They use their knowledge and expertise to assess the direction novices are heading and to create opportunities and conditions that support meaningful teacher learning in the service of student learning.[37]

In her single case study of an "articulate" mentor, Feiman-Nemser gives numerous examples from her interviews and observations of the kind of mentoring that, she maintains, "cultivates a disposition of inquiry, focusing attention on student thinking and understanding, and fostering disciplined talk about problems of practice."[38] This mentor did not pose as an expert, rather choosing to cothink with the new teacher, model target behaviors, and focus on instructional issues that the new teacher would not have seen by herself.

Steve Athanases and Betty Achinstein examined data from new teachers and mentors who participated in a learning network. Through questionnaires and reviews of two sets of mentor-teacher conversations they showed that mentors can move new teachers beyond their initial inclination for survival support toward an examination of the needs of the student learners, particularly the low performers. The mentors accomplish this with a focus on student assessment, alignment of curriculum with standards, and ongoing formative assessment of the beginning teachers.[39]

With her colleague Adele Barrett, Betty Achinstein analyzed data on 15 mentors and their teachers who were working with culturally and linguistically diverse elementary students.[40] Referring to the literature on novice teachers and teachers in training, they started with the assumption that new teachers tend to view their students from a managerial frame of reference, focusing on issues of behavior control and maintaining order.[41] Achinstein and Barrett found that, to differing degrees, mentors were able to help their mentees move beyond a primarily managerial focus so that they "reframed" their perspectives on students to include both a human relations frame that spotlights classroom social systems, individual student needs, and interrelationships among students, as well as a political frame that takes account of inequalities and power differentials, and sees classrooms as settings for social change. Their analysis of mentor-teacher conversations revealed that it was not always easy for mentors to effect this philosophical reframing, as they were confronted with differing beliefs from the beginning teachers and the prevailing school cultures.

In my own study with Wendy Baron of mentoring conversations, I found that mentors trained in the NTC model tended to emphasize indirectness in the way they made suggestions to the beginning teachers in their caseloads.[42] Perhaps motivated by a desire to minimize the power differential in an expert-novice relationship, mentors adopted various linguistic strategies to avoid giving direct instructions to their mentees. In over 30 hours of conversations about observed lessons we identified only 10 examples of direct suggestions. Furthermore, fully two thirds of the mentors' suggestions produced no elaborated responses from the beginning teachers: This suggests that the mentor's input often did not provoke them to think in depth about their teaching practice.

Another study comparing these same California mentor-teacher conversations with conversations recorded in China focused on the content of the discussions.[43] The findings revealed that Chinese mentors talked more about subject matter content and less about individual students than U.S. mentors. Also unlike U.S. mentors, they dominated the conversations and often made direct suggestions, which were elaborated with reasons and examples. These differences probably reflect international differences in curriculum, mentor training and expectations, and possibly cultural differences regarding interpersonal communication.

Other studies have polled beginning teachers to find out what they value most from their mentoring and induction programs. These suggest that teachers value having postobservation reflecting discussions about their teaching,[44] observing and being observed,[45] and receiving support with classroom management, lesson planning, and relationships with students.[46] Our own surveys of induction program participants conducted at the NTC bear out these findings. With some differences among contexts, teachers typically value support with classroom management, lesson planning, student assessment, resources, and differentiating instruction to address the needs of all students. Emotional support is valued also.

ASSESSING THE EVIDENCE: WHAT KINDS OF MENTORING AND INDUCTION ARE AVAILABLE FOR BEGINNING TEACHERS?

From the above overview of high-profile induction and mentoring programs we can see that there is a variety of options to teachers in different parts of the country and the world. Of course, these formal descriptions represent the programs' ideal types, which may diverge from their on-the-ground representations in any given school or setting and for any particular teacher. We cannot assume that implementation necessarily reflects the formal specifications of the programs.

A body of research has focused on what goes on when mentors work with beginning teachers. When new teachers are surveyed, they are likely to report that they are grateful for whatever support they are getting, and when the process itself is investigated, we find evidence that mentors are able to influence teachers toward so-called reform-minded instruction.

It remains to be seen whether and to what extent induction and mentoring programs for beginning teachers are effective and worth the time and money that governments, states, and schools invest in them. Beyond the simple question of whether teachers are satisfied with the program,[47] there are more interesting issues: Are new teachers who receive induction support less likely to drop out of teaching than those who don't? What effects does participation in an induction program have on new teachers' classroom practice? Does teacher participation in an induction program have a positive effect on their students' achievement? Are teacher induction programs cost-effective? The remainder of this book will consider these questions through a critical review of the existing research.

Chapter 3

Induction Programs and Teacher Retention

A lot of work has been done on teacher movement into and out of various schools and out of teaching altogether. Researchers have studied who enters teaching, who stays in teaching, and who quits teaching and why. They're studied the rates at which teachers leave schools and the profession, and the plans currently employed teachers have for staying or leaving. Some of these studies focus on beginning teachers—for they are the most vulnerable to attrition—and whether support from a mentor or an induction program appears to have any effect on their decisions not to quit.

DEFINITIONS

Before we begin to look at this literature, we need to be clear on the terminology. *Retention,* and its antonym *attrition,* are not clearly drawn concepts when they are used to refer to teachers. First, and most important, we must distinguish between retention in the teaching profession and retention at a particular school or district. Second, we should be clear about what we mean when we classify someone as *teacher.* In other words, are we including uncertified teachers, part-time or substitute teachers, interns, fellows, members of programs such as Teach for America, and teachers in training, as well as those with full-time positions and full certification? Likewise, definition of the term *beginning teacher* may vary. In some settings it refers only to first-year teachers, in others to teachers in their first two or three years. In at least one case, researchers defined beginning teachers as in those who had been teaching 10 or fewer years.[1] The period of retention is also important. Are we looking only at those teachers who quit during a given year, or are we measuring a more substantial period of time such as 5 to 10 years?

A variety of labels are used for the different concepts associated with teacher mobility. For example, the expression "turnover" may apply both to movement among schools or to departure from the profession. Similarly, *retention* can mean remaining in a school or district, or staying in the profession.[2] Richard Ingersoll makes the distinction through use of the term *migration* for movement among schools and *attrition* for movement out of the profession. Others[3] refer to *movers* (for those changing schools), *leavers* (for teachers leaving the profession), and *stayers* (for those remaining in the same school). Some[4] further identify movement within a school district (*reassignment*) as distinct from movement to another school district (*migration*). Another comparison is made by some between *turnover* (used to describe movement among schools), and *wastage*, which refers to departure from the profession (this last term may be localized to users of British English).[5] In the fields of sociology or economics "mobility" is frequently used as a synonym for "turnover,"[6] while some economists[7] also use the term "transition" to refer to movement out of a school district and out of the state (but not necessarily out of teaching). In this book any of these terms may be used, depending on the research under review. However, I will generally adopt the NCTAF terminology, and use "movers and leavers" to distinguish those who change schools from those who quit the profession, and "stayers," for want of a more elegant term, to refer to those who stay put.

WHO ENTERS THE TEACHING PROFESSION?

A 2005 U.S. Department of Education report entitled *Mobility in the Teacher Workforce* written by Stephen Provasnick and Scott Dorfman for the National Center for Educational Statistics (NCES) has the following descriptive statistics about teachers working in the 1999–2000 school year, drawn from the SASS database:

- About 3,450,000 teachers (excluding kindergarten teachers and teacher aides) worked in public and private elementary and secondary schools across the country—representing about 2.7% of the overall U.S. workforce that year.
- Elementary and secondary school teachers constituted a greater percentage of the workforce than physicians (0.5%), legal professionals (0.8%), postsecondary faculty (0.9%), engineers (1.0%), firemen and law enforcement workers (1.0%), registered nurses (1.5%), or any other professional group that year.

- Elementary and secondary school teachers constituted about the same percentage of the workforce as all secretaries and administrative assistants (2.7%) and slightly less than retail workers (2.8%).
- The majority of teachers (90%) worked full-time, 4% worked part-time, 3% were itinerant teachers, and less than 0.5% worked as long-term substitutes. Eighty-seven percent worked in public schools, and 13% in private schools.
- Seventy-five percent of the teachers were female, similar in both public and private schools. However, the distribution of teachers by sex differed widely by grade level. Among elementary grade teachers, 91% were female. In contrast, at the high school level only 55% were female, and in the middle grades the proportion was 73%.
- The average brand-new teacher was 29 years old (the median age was 26), suggesting that many teachers do not enter the teacher workforce right out of college. The average age of all teachers was 42 (the median was 44); about 29% were under age 35, 42% were ages 35–49, and 29% were 50 or older.[8]

Anyone who has been in a K–12 school knows that more women than men become teachers, especially at the lower grades.[9] However, the degree of this imbalance has been declining over the years. In 1960 fully 50% of female college graduates chose to enter teaching compared to just 10% in 1990.[10] Data from SASS surveys showed that 78% of new teachers in 1987–88 were women, versus 73% in 1993–94.[11] Now we see from the most recent NCES data that 75% of public school teachers were women in the 1999–2000 school year, so maybe the downward trend has stopped.[12]

Whereas the proportion of female teachers has declined, the proportion of White non-Hispanic teachers seems to be fairly constant (after an interim rise), in spite of a sharp increase in minority student enrollment. In 1972, 78% of K–12 students were White compared to 58% in 2005.[13] In 1987–88, 91.3% of all teachers were categorized as White non-Hispanic; in 1990–91 the figure was 88.8%; in 1993, 84%.[14] Ten years later the most recent government figures for 2003–04 showed that the percentage of White non-Hispanic teachers was still 83.7%.[15] June Gordon interviewed 140 minority teachers over a 2-year period in Cincinnati, Ohio, in Seattle, Washington, and in Long Beach, California, during the early 1990s.[16] In the opinion of her minority teacher informants, students of color were reluctant to enter teaching not only because of the low pay, as previous studies[17] had reported, but because of negative experiences in school, lack of adequate academic preparation, poor counseling, and the negative status of teaching. The most revealing reason, according to Gordon, was that students of color across the board were discouraged from entering teaching. Gordon provides little information about her informants, however, so it is difficult to generalize from her findings, which by now may be somewhat out-of-date.[18] Also problematic is the fact that minorities who had chosen to become teachers were asked for their opinions about why others had opted not to enter that profession; more compelling would have been data from the members of the very group that had rejected the teaching option. Furthermore, other researchers, albeit with smaller samples, have received different feedback from their minority informants, who report that their families did indeed encourage them to pursue teaching.[19]

It has been a common refrain for many years that teaching is not attracting "the best and brightest" of our young people,[20] even though we know that students learn more from teachers with strong academic skills.[21] This is confirmed by a number of studies suggesting that college graduates in the top quartile of academic ability (as measured, for example, by ACT scores, college entrance examination (CEE) scores, or Praxis I and II test results) were half as likely to enter teaching than college graduates in the bottom quartile.[22] Also, those in the top quartile are more than twice as likely than teachers in the bottom quartile to teach in private schools and are less than one third as likely as teachers in the bottom quartile to teach in high poverty schools.[23] Another study demonstrated that graduates of higher quality (i.e., more selective)[24] institutions were less likely to choose a teaching major and less likely to choose to teach than graduates of lower quality institutions.[25] Such findings satisfy the labor market supply-and-demand predictions of economists, who see human decision-making behavior in terms of the opportunity costs of deciding on a given option. Thus individuals who have access to attractive alternatives to teaching would be less likely to enter the profession than those with fewer desirable options. People with a more idealistic vision of teaching as a profession might consider a different set of motivations. For example, noneconomic factors such as a desire for social justice or an intrinsic love of children and of the work may be more salient[26] (although these could also be factored into the opportunity cost equation as intrinsic rewards).

WHO STAYS, WHO MOVES, AND WHO LEAVES?

The 2005 NCES report, cited in the previous section, published the following statistics regarding teacher turnover in 1999–2000:

- At the end of the year, about 16% of the teacher workforce "turned over" or did not continue teaching in the same school during the next school year. About half of teacher turnover can be attributed to the transfer of teachers between schools.
- The turnover was larger at the end of 1999–2000 than at the end of 1987–88, 1990–91, or 1993–94 (16% versus 14%, 13%, and 14%, respectively).
- Teachers transfer at higher rates to public schools than to private schools. Public school teachers in high-poverty schools are twice as likely as their counterparts in low-poverty public schools to transfer to another school.
- The percentage of teachers who retired at the end of the school year was small relative to rates of total turnover: only 2% out of 16%.
- The percentage of teachers who left teaching for a job outside elementary or secondary teaching at the end of 1999–2000 was twice as large as that of teachers who retired (4% v versus 2%). Teachers who took a job other than elementary or secondary teaching were disproportionately male compared with continuing teachers.
- Less than 2% left teaching for family reasons, to return to school, or for other reasons at the end of 1999–2000. Virtually all teachers who left for family reasons were female. Teachers who left to return to school had an average of 4 years of teaching experience.
- About a quarter of newly hired teachers in 1999–2000 (4% out of 17%) were returning teachers.
- Private school teachers are more likely to leave teaching than public school teachers.[27]

The most common finding from studies of movement out of the teaching profession is that attrition is high for new teachers, lower for more experienced teachers, and then high again as teachers move toward retirement, depicted by a U-shaped curve.[28] Xiaofeng Liu further analyzed the attrition rates of new teachers using the 1999–2000 SASS data and found that first-year teachers are 3% more likely to quit than other teachers over a one-year period.[29] Jianping Shen and Louann Palmer analyzed national data from the Baccalaureate and Beyond Longitudinal study, 1993–1997 (BAB), and determined that 34% of those who entered teaching quit by the end of the fifth year.[30] They also found that those with inadequate preparation (i.e., would-be teachers who did not complete student teaching, receive certification, or participate in a teacher induction program) were more likely to drop out. Other researchers who analyzed the BAB reported similar findings.[31] One study examined teacher attrition rates in the state of California during the 1990s; the authors found that 13% of teachers had left public schools by the end of their second year and 22% had quit by the end of their fourth year.[32]

Women teachers have higher attrition rates than men[33] (and this may be due partially to child-rearing issues);[34] Whites have higher attrition rates than minorities[35] (although one study suggested that Latino teachers were equally likely to change roles within the field of education),[36] and teachers with higher abilities are more likely to quit than the rest.[37] Some leavers return after a break, particularly women who take time off to have a child.[38]

Similar to the finding that students from higher status universities are less likely to choose teaching as a profession, Dick Murnane and Randall Olsen's research on data from North Carolina that shows teachers with the highest level of general skills, as measured by scores on a standardized test such as the National Teachers Exam (NTE), are more likely to leave. Once again the principle of opportunity cost is in operation. Murnane and Olsen added to this finding the assumption that some college graduates obtain teacher certification as a fairly low-cost hedge against the possibility of not finding a good job outside of teaching.[39] The plausibility of the market hedge assumption is supported by other evidence, namely, that 40% of the individuals who obtained teacher certification in North Carolina between 1975 and 1985 never taught in that state's public schools.[40] In a recent working paper, Dan Goldhaber and colleagues revisit this question and show quite the opposite conclusion. They examined attrition and mobility of teachers using student achievement outcomes for early-career teachers in North Carolina public schools from 1996 to 2002. Their findings suggest that the most effective teachers tend to stay in teaching and in specific schools and, contrary to expectations from previous research, more effective teachers are not more likely to leave more challenging schools.[41]

Early studies comparing attrition rates across different occupations produced conflicting, or at best inconclusive findings,[42] until Doug Harris and Scott Adams analyzed a large set of pooled data from the Current Population Survey (CPS) from 1992–2001, and clarified some of the apparent contradictions.[43] Richard Ingersoll had concluded from his analysis of SASS data that turnover among teachers was higher than for other professions (as represented by data from other researchers). Robin Henke and Lisa Zahn, on the other hand, using figures from the BAB, determined that, after 3 years in the profession, teachers were less likely to quit work than were college graduates in other professions.[44] This difference may be explained by the fact that Ingersoll looked at turnover rates throughout the teachers' careers and used a group of nurses as a comparison, whereas Henke and Zahn focused only on teachers' first three years of work. Also, other researchers compared them to college graduates in all professions. However, one of Ingersoll's conclusions was that turnover rates for teachers were indeed much higher in the early years, and retirement was not such a big drain; efforts, therefore, should be made to stem the flow of this "leaky bucket."[45]

Todd Stinebrickner conducted a third study using yet another database, the National Longitudinal Survey (NLS). He compared the attrition from the labor force of teachers with that of other college graduates during their first ten years out of school. From his small, but rich, data set he determined that the number of teachers who quit work altogether formed a much higher percentage of the turnover of teachers than for those in other professions.[46]

With this history of somewhat contradictory findings as a background, Harris and Adams compared attrition rates for teachers, nurses, social workers, and accountants. Their extensive analysis produces a number of findings, which themselves are complex enough sometimes to appear contradictory. At the risk of oversimplifying, it is worth summarizing some of their results:

1. There is a 7.73% chance that a teacher will leave the profession in any given year.
2. This is higher than the rate for nurses (consistent with Ingersoll's findings) but lower than that for the other professions.
3. A 10% increase in salary reduces teacher attrition by almost 5%.
4. When worker characteristics are controlled for, female teachers are less prone to turnover than males (contrary to conventional wisdom).
5. Overall turnover rates by age show the familiar U-shaped curve for teachers, but the curve is steeper at the older age levels.
6. Teachers are more likely than others to take early retirement, possibly because of relatively high pension-to-salary ratios.
7. *Average* turnover rates for teachers are no higher than for the other professions.[47]

Harris and Adams' finding that 7.73% of teachers leave the profession compares with Ingersoll's analysis from the SASS/TFS data (7.9% in the 1987–88 school year, and 7.6% in 1990–91, to 9% in 1993–94). This level of agreement between data sets from the two different sources suggests that an estimate of a 7–8% turnover rate has a good chance of being valid (it is also close to the numbers reported from California data). However, their finding that teachers tend to take early retirement, thus causing the attrition rate to be higher among older teachers, is in direct contradiction to Ingersoll's findings. Also this trend is not found in the other professions they examined. They suggest that high pension-salary ratios for teachers may explain this phenomenon.

WHY TEACHERS QUIT

From an economist's point of view, why teachers move or leave is another question that may be answered by weighing their present job against alternatives that are more attractive in terms of compensation, working conditions, or intrinsic rewards.

The 2005 NCES report already cited included the following findings related to teachers' reasons for moving or leaving:

- Teachers who left at the end of 1999–2000 most commonly identified retirement (20%) as a reason for leaving teaching, followed by family reasons (16%), pregnancy/child rearing (14%), wanting a better salary and benefits (14%), and wanting to pursue a different kind of career (13%).
- Teachers who either left teaching or transferred at the end of 1999–2000 reported a lack of planning time, too heavy a workload, too low a salary, and problematic student behavior among their top five sources of dissatisfaction with the school they left.[48]

Other researchers investigating why teachers move or leave have uncovered a long list of reasons, across a panoply of studies of varying levels of sophistication: inadequate salary and incentives;[49] lack of or inadequate support from administration;[50] lack of support from colleagues;[51] lack of support from community and parents;[52] stress;[53] lure of competitive fields outside education;[54] age;[55] problems with subject area assignment;[56] wrong grade-level assignment;[57] lack of opportunity for professional development;[58] violence and safety;[59] inadequate training and preparation;[60] funding inequities or lack of resources;[61] large class size;[62] lack of decision-making ability;[63] extra duties and/or time demands;[64] burdens of bureaucracy or school policy, expressed as lack of time to confer with colleagues, lack of privacy, an inability to make phone calls, lack of access to the school building, prescheduled break and lunch time, and requirements to document hours.[65]

Broadly speaking, this laundry list of reasons why teachers are not satisfied with their current positions refers either to poor pay or to some aspect or effect of their working conditions. Which of these general categories is more salient in teachers' decisions to stay or leave is the focus of a body of research from the United States and Europe, conducted mostly by economists who are interested in to what degree financial reward, relative to other factors, affects teacher recruitment and mobility. Early work on data from North Carolina and Michigan,[66] and later studies from the United Kingdom,[67] found that higher teacher salaries are associated with lower rates of attrition from the profession. Another group of researchers examined transfer among districts in the state of Washington, and found that teachers were more likely to move when salaries are increased statewide, or when administrative spending is high.[68] Others who reviewed national CPS data followed exiting teachers to their newly assumed professions, and estimated that the probability of a teacher quitting decreases by 2.11% if salaries are increased by 1%. Their analysis is based on the human capital theory of occupational choice, which posits that individuals make systematic assessment of benefits and costs of entering and staying in a profession. Others also rely on this theory, in order to explain the fact that younger teachers are more likely to leave because they have yet to build up an accumulation of specific human capital.[69] I've already noted that Harris and Adams concluded from their statistical analysis of CPS data that a 10% salary increase reduces attrition by a more conservative 5%.[70]

Todd Stinebrickner, also using national data, estimated that new teachers were more responsive to wages than improved working conditions, such as smaller class size, in their decisions to stay in teaching.[71] In a second study using proportional hazard models,[72] Stinebrickner showed that a 25% salary raise would increase the duration of beginning teachers' careers by 50%.[73] Jennifer Imazeki, also an economist, examined the effects of salary increases for teachers in Wisconsin. She tested various wage increase scenarios and concluded that increasing salaries could indeed help alleviate shortages by increasing the retention of beginning teachers.[74]

Other economists such as Dale Ballou and Michael Podgursky have gone even further by suggesting that pay-for-performance and dismissal strategies should be introduced in public schools in order to improve retention. They base this on the finding that private schools, where there is greater salary flexibility, appear to retain their better qualified teachers more successfully than public schools.[75] Yet other economists, Eric Hanushek and his colleagues, had problems with these findings because of potential correlations between working conditions (such as class size and student characteristics) and salary, that may account for the transitions that the other researchers observed. Their own results from Texas data indicated that student characteristics such as race and achievement were more strongly related to teacher mobility than salary, which had only a modest effect once compensating differentials were taken into account.[76] Data from Norwegian primary and secondary schools bear this out: Researchers found that in Norway teachers tend to leave schools with high percentages of minority students and students with special needs. They also found that retention rates were greater in larger schools and in schools that had large numbers of teachers without certification, but recognized that these may be proxies for other variables that may make a school less appealing to teachers.[77]

A study comparing class-load factors with financial and other personal and district characteristics among teachers in the state of New York found that factors such as class size, number of classes taught, student quality, and percentage of class time spent out of a teacher's certification area were important correlates of teacher movement, either to other positions or out of the profession.[78]

Nancy Latham and Paul Vogt conducted a longitudinal study of attrition in Illinois public schools among graduates from one institute of higher education over the period from 1996 through 2003. Their goal was to test whether teachers prepared in Professional Development Schools (PDSs) were more likely to enter and remain in teaching than those whose preparation had been in non-PDSs. They found that, while controlling for student background and cognitive characteristics, teachers who received their preparation in a PDS were more likely to enter and persist in teaching than those prepared in regular schools.[79]

Richard Ingersoll examined the sources of teacher turnover using data from the Schools and Staffing Survey (SASS) and its supplement, the Teacher Follow-up Survey (TFS). His analysis showed that, of teachers who quit because they are dissatisfied, 54% stated that their salaries were too low, 43% felt a lack of administrative support, 23% were unable to handle student discipline problems, and 15% were disenchanted with the lack of student motivation. Lack of opportunity for professional advancement, inadequate preparation time, intrusions on teaching time, and large class size were the remaining factors.[80] A similar number of teachers departed in search of another job or career, which might also reflect a motivation for higher pay.[81]

Xiaofeng Liu, using the same data set, assessed the effect of teachers' participation in school decision making on first-year teachers' decisions to stay or leave. Liu used the seven SASS questionnaire items that asked teachers to rate teacher influence over school policy at their schools on a 5-point scale. The seven items surveyed teacher influence over standards for students, curriculum, professional development, teacher evaluation, new hires, discipline policy, and school budget. Liu determined that teacher influence over school policy at school can mitigate first-year teachers' propensity to leave the teaching profession: The predicted probability of first-year teacher attrition can decrease from 19% to 4% as teacher influence at school changes from no influence to a great deal of influence. The covariation between teacher influence and teacher tendency to stay in the teaching profession suggests that teacher participation in school decision-making has a positive effect on their professional lives. This finding supports those teacher leadership programs that advocate for teachers' involvement in school decision making.[82]

A study by Jianping Shen, very similar to Ingersoll's but less often cited (even by Ingersoll), had appeared four years earlier.[83] Shen analyzed the same SASS and TFS databases to study teacher retention and attrition, the only difference from the Ingersoll study being that he restricted his examination to public schools. Shen's findings both "confirm and challenge" those reported in earlier research. He confirmed that less-experienced teachers are more likely to move or leave, that salary is correlated with teacher retention, that appreciation for the intrinsic merits of the teaching profession helps teachers remain, and that empowering teachers by giving them influence over school policies is also associated with retention. He also discovered that teachers tended to leave poor schools with larger numbers of minority students, a finding that foreshadows Hanushek's conclusion that race and achievement were more strongly related to teacher mobility than salary.[84] Furthermore, the location of the school was not associated with retention or attrition, contrary to the findings of other studies that had indicated that teachers tend to leave good schools in wealthy communities, possibly a reflection of school busing patterns or the inclusion of private school data.[85]

Stress, expressed as tension, frustration, anxiety, anger or depression, is another factor, a derivative of working conditions, that has been posited to cause teachers to quit.[86] The authors of an ILO-UNESCO report claimed that 25-33% of teachers suffered significantly from stress, and argued that this was one of the major reasons that teachers quit the profession.[87] In another study stress was engendered in special education teachers who, because of administrative pressures for performance efficiency, did not develop a sense that they were influencing student learning, and therefore felt that what they were doing did not matter.[88] Expressing the same idea in terms of internal versus external locus of control and intrinsic motivation, other researchers noted that performance efficiency is also affected by the psychic rewards or positive feedback from principals and colleagues. Together, the negative effects of extrinsic motivation and low psychic rewards can increase stress and lead to attrition.[89] Given appropriate supervision and positive communication, however, the effects of teacher stress can be ameliorated.[90]

Special education teachers have also been studied with regard to their attrition and retention rates.[91] Special education teachers tend to quit at greater rates than teachers in general education, and are inclined to be more dissatisfied,[92] and burned out.[93] Bonnie Billingsley conducted a valuable review of this work. Definitions of retention and attrition vary among the studies, as do their samples and their methodologies. However, they suggest a stable set of findings. Special education teachers who quit tend to be younger and inexperienced, uncertified, have higher than average test scores, and are influenced by personal factors such as children or family moves. Those who stay do so because of higher salaries, a positive school climate, good support systems, opportunities for professional development, and reasonable role demands. When these conditions are not present, teachers show increased stress, develop negative reactions to work, have low levels of satisfaction and commitment, and ultimately they quit.[94]

Russell Gersten and colleagues studied special education teachers in three large urban districts. They used path analysis[95] to look at the relation between intention to stay in teaching and factors such as job satisfaction and commitment, and found that stress due to job design (a concept borrowed from occupational research related to feasibility) had a negative effect that could be partly reversed by principal and collegial support.[96]

Other researchers have looked at factors unrelated either to working conditions or pay. For example, Linda Darling-Hammond, in her report for NCTAF, examined the relation between different pathways to teaching and retention in the profession.[97] She found that retention was related to higher levels of preparation. Eighty-four percent of those teachers with a subject-matter BA and an MA in teaching were still teaching after 3 years, compared to 53% of those with a 4-year degree only (whether in a subject-matter field or in education) and only 34% who had attended a short-term alternative certification program in addition to a BA. Her opinion is that these alternative routes to teaching exacerbate the supply-and-demand problems rather than alleviate them, implying that less comprehensive preparation leads to early attrition. However, alternative certification programs may vary in quality and/or in their goals (consider Teach For America, for example, where participants agree to teach for 2 years only, although some remain longer).

Martin Haberman, on the other hand, reports on the efforts of the Milwaukee Public Schools (MPS) to recruit and retain minority teachers for the long term, and finds positive correlations with retention. In collaboration with a teachers' association and a local university, MPS formed an alternative teacher education program whereby minority candidates with a bachelor's degree are given summer training in teaching followed by a year of residency with a mentor. Haberman reports that 94% of those that complete the program stayed in the MPS system over a 10-year period of study.[98]

An alternative perspective is adopted by Sonia Nieto. Rather than focusing on why teachers quit, she examines why teachers stay, or, as she puts it,

> what keeps dedicated teachers in the classroom, particularly the most enthusiastic and unbeaten among them. In other words, what helps good public school teachers persevere, in spite of all deprivations and challenges?[99]

Her conclusion is that a fundamental love of the work causes teachers to remain in their classrooms, even under the harshest and most challenging conditions. In other words, her belief is that emotional and personal factors can trump the exigencies of poor working conditions and low salaries. Her findings, it should be noted, were drawn from a one-year close study of a small group of "excellent" high school teachers. There was no comparison group, no random selection, and no attempt to make the data generalizable.

Susan Moore Johnson and her graduate student colleagues at Harvard followed 50 first- and second-year teachers over 4 years. Through regular in-depth interviews with ten of these teachers the researchers collected detailed information leading them to argue that the nature of the teaching career and the labor market has changed for our present generation of teachers. With alternative, nontraditional pathways into the profession and expectations for a decent salary, administrative support, collegial environment, and opportunities for advancement, today's teachers—without an inbuilt intention to commit to a lifetime in any one occupation—are liable to move or quit more readily than teachers of previous generations.[100]

In a recent addition to this literature, Karen Quartz and her colleagues at UCLA examined 6-year longitudinal data from the gradu-

ates of their teacher preparation program that focuses on social justice and urban education.[101] From survey responses of 838 teachers
out of 1,084 that had graduated from the program from 2000 to 2005,
they found that a significant amount of turnover could be described as
"role changing." By creating "survival models" or "event histories"
that plotted if and when attrition happened, they modeled two attrition options or hazard probabilities: teachers who left for a job outside
of education, and teachers who left full-time classroom teaching for
a job inside education (the role-changing group). Their data showed
that, by the eighth career year, 70% of accumulated teacher attrition
was due to role changes. Role changes referred to positions in administration, part-time or substitute teacher, or other educational positions
inside or outside the K–12 school district. They also found that 95% of
graduates in their third year had been teaching consistently, a proportion that dropped to 68% by the time they reached their seventh year.
About three quarters of the sample remained in classroom teaching
over their entire career pathway (stayers), while the remaining quarter
changed roles, or left and returned to the classroom one or more times.
This study adds a dimension to the understanding of teacher turnover
and attrition by focusing on role changes within education, and it highlights the potential weakness of research that looks at data only from a
single year in that it would identify role changers and those who leave
but plan to return as leavers.

Overall, these studies bring to light a range of reasons why teachers
change schools or leave teaching, with context often being the factor
that determines which variable may be most critical. Of course teachers also quit for non-job-related personal reasons, such as pregnancy,
relocation for spouse's work, medical issues, or changes in a family's
financial situation. They may also quit because they move to other
educational positions such as administrator or university professor,
because they are fired, or because they retire. One thing that is not discussed across all these studies is that some teachers quit because they
don't feel competent. Since the data originate largely from self-report
questionnaires, it is not surprising that this information does not surface. Either it is not one of the questions on the survey (for good reason), or teachers do not volunteer this motivation for quitting in their
open-ended responses. Surely, it must be a factor for some percentage
of those who decide to give up teaching.

Induction and mentoring programs may help beginning teachers
compensate for imperfect working conditions, but are irrelevant regarding personal issues. For teachers struggling with competency, induction support may help them improve their skills, or mentors may

rightfully counsel them out of the profession. These factors should be taken into account when assessing rates of beginning teacher attrition and retention, and any potential effects of induction programs.

METHODOLOGY FOR EXAMINING ATTRITION AND RETENTION RATES

Studies of teacher retention and attrition are conducted using one of two fundamental methodological approaches: *multivariate* or *bivariate*. In the *multivariate* approach, researchers inquire into a set of variables simultaneously in order to test hypotheses about why individuals choose to stay in or leave a given profession. Researchers who use a multivariate design sometimes start from a theoretical perspective, such as the human capital theory of Sheila Kirby and David Grissmer.[102] These authors explain teacher retention rates by positing that teachers make cost-benefit decisions about staying or leaving motivated by the amount of human capital they have invested. The greater the investment, the less likely teachers are to quit. In another multivariate study, based on a theoretical approach that considered teachers as "economically rational decision makers who choose among alternatives to rationalize their utility," Neil Theobald found that teachers' decisions to stay or leave a particular school district were negatively related to local property values and positively associated with salary.[103]

From the perspective of social learning theory, David Chapman and colleagues studied four groups of individuals with teaching certificates. Some taught full-time, some sporadically, some had quit, and the others had never taught. After identifying differences among the four groups in factors such as personal characteristics, commitment levels, and degree of satisfaction, the researchers found that differences in retention and attrition could be explained as a process of social learning. The significance of their work is in the importance attached to factors "outside the influence of school administrators or of teacher preparation programs."[104] However, they note in their second report that "additionally, results from this study underscore the importance (to retention) of current work conditions, which can be influenced by school administrators."[105]

Ingersoll looks at the issue from the perspective of the sociology of organizations in his analyses of the 1999–2001 cycle of SASS and TFS surveys.[106] His premise is that turnover affects organizational performance and effectiveness while it, in turn, is affected by the character and conditions of the organization, requiring therefore that one examine turnover from the perspective of the organization.[107]

Rather than test any particular theory, some multivariate studies simply include a number of potentially important variables in the analysis, based on what has been learned from previous work. Thus Shen examined three types of variables in his analysis of data from the 1991 SASS and the 1992 TFS: personal characteristics, school characteristics, and teachers' perceptions.[108] Personal characteristics included such items as number of years teaching, salary, and race. School characteristics covered issues concerning the school, staff, and student demographics, whether there was a mentoring program, and the way classes were organized. Teachers' perceptions included variables related to their feelings about the school's problems, the administration, and student behavior.

In the more commonly found *bivariate* approach, researchers test the relationship between retention or attrition and one other variable. As I have already shown, many different variables have been associated with teachers' decisions to stay or leave, most of which are related either to salary or to working conditions, but include personal factors. The "other" variable of interest in this book is induction support, or the lack of it.

APPROACHES TO MEASURING THE EFFECTS OF INDUCTION SUPPORT ON TEACHER RETENTION

Many reports describe or prescribe the content of induction programs. That programs with a great variety of elements have been developed is well documented in an assortment of reports and articles, in addition to the most widely known programs described in Chapter 2.[109] The majority of research on the effects of induction and mentoring on teacher retention has been conducted at the program level. There are essentially two approaches to measuring retention rates at the program level. One can either follow new teachers longitudinally for a period of time and track who stays and who leaves, or one can take a retroactive look at the records of teachers who started their careers at a given time in the past, find out where they are now, and calculate the retention rates. In either case, it is necessary to have access to school district human resource files (which, even when they have the necessary information about teachers' years of experience, are often unreliable). It is also important to be able to make comparisons among groups of teachers who receive different levels of induction support.

An alternative to studying teacher induction programs individually is to analyze information about teachers' self-reported experiences with induction from a large database such as the SASS/TFS. In this case, induction is one of many variables under review, and the duration of retention is measurable over a one-year time period only.

It is also worth noting that some researchers measure actual retention by looking at statistics of teacher turnover, while others estimate turnover by canvassing teachers' *intentions* regarding whether they will stay in or leave their current teaching positions. The following research review covers studies that use both multivariate and bivariate methodologies, and those with actual and planned retention information.

STUDIES OF HOW INDUCTION AND MENTORING AFFECT TEACHER RETENTION

There are many research reports of studies examining new teacher attrition and induction support.[110] Some of these appear in peer-reviewed journals or book chapters, some in less academic publications, some as internal reports, and some as dissertations. Richard Ingersoll and his graduate student Jeff Kralik surveyed approximately 150 empirical studies of teacher induction and mentoring that had been conducted prior to 2004, in order to determine their effects on teacher retention. I want to begin with a detailed discussion of their review.[111] They established three criteria for including studies in their overview: Researchers must have collected quantitative data, they must have evaluated induction effects and produced outcomes, and they should have included comparisons of effects and outcomes with those of non-mentored teachers. Having run the literature search through these filters, Ingersoll and Kralik were left with just ten studies. These studies, the authors conclude, "do provide empirical support for the claim that assistance for new teachers, and, in particular, mentoring programs have a positive effect on teachers and their retention." However, Ingersoll and Kralik also identified two rather substantial weaknesses in the studies. The first problem was that none of the researchers included any control for other factors that might have affected the outcomes, and the second was that the programs varied so much from site to site that it is not possible to generalize the findings of any single study. The reader is encouraged to bear these shortcomings in mind when considering any of the research reviewed here.

On closer inspection, one finds further limitations among the ten studies that made Ingersoll and Kralik's cut. Three of the studies, for example, did not measure actual retention, but rather gathered information about teachers' professional intentions and future plans.[112] Ingersoll and Kralik do acknowledge that findings would be "more solid" if actual retention data had been collected, a somewhat generous assessment of a claim that hypothetical retention is an adequate indicator of actual retention. Two of the other studies measured retention after only one year of teaching,[113] and another examined volunteer (i.e., unpaid) mentors.[114] Thus, despite the rigorous selection criteria of Ingersoll and Kralik, the majority include features that might be considered to compromise their findings. Of the four remaining studies, two were conducted by Ingersoll himself,[115] one by Sandra Odell and Douglas Ferraro,[116] and the last by Ed Fuller.[117] Tom Smith and Richard Ingersoll wrote a follow-up report to their study of the 1999-2000 SASS data that was published in 2004.[118]

Ingersoll and his colleagues conducted thorough analyses of the SASS and TFS for 1990–1991 and 1999–2000. In his examination of the earlier set of SASS data, Ingersoll found that having a mentoring program, per se, did not lead to increased teacher satisfaction, whereas assistance that was simply *described* as effective "had a strong positive effect." Using this finding, Ingersoll then examined the relationship between effective assistance and actual teacher turnover, finding that beginning teachers who reported having had effective assistance showed a 92% lower rate of departure from the school either for another position or to quit the profession altogether. The main limitation of this study is, of course, the lack of an objective definition of effective assistance. Further, since teachers who are generally satisfied may be likely to rate the quality of their assistance positively, while unhappy teachers will probably do the opposite, effective assistance may be a proxy for other factors not included in the multivariate analysis.[119]

In a subsequent, widely read report, Smith and Ingersoll address the limitations of the earlier study, and consider the cumulative effects of various induction components on one-year retention. They identify "basic induction" as having a mentor in supportive communication with administrators; one level up is "basic induction plus collaboration," which adds new teacher seminars and either common planning time or collaboration with other teachers; next comes "basic induction plus collaboration plus teacher network plus extra resources," where participation in an external teacher network, a reduced number of preparations, and a teacher's aide are added to the other types of support. Only 1% of the beginning teachers in their dataset had the full package, 26% had the next level of support, 56% had basic induction, and 3% had no induction at all. They demonstrated that the greater the number of induction components the lower were the turnover rates for both movers and leavers after one year of teaching. However, the attrition rates for those teachers who had received basic induction (18% leavers and 21% movers) were barely different from those who had had no induction (20% leavers and 21% movers). At the next level of induction support the numbers went down to 12% and 15%. Only 9% of the few teachers who received the full package quit the profession, and another 9% transferred to other schools.[120]

Of the ten studies, those conducted by Ingersoll and colleagues (and also the one by Shen)[121] that use the SASS databases have the largest sample sizes and use the most sophisticated quantitative analyses. However, one potential problem with these large databases concerns the weighted sampling approach. This can result in accentuating non-response effects, leading to the possibility that some of the subgroups may not be representative of in the general population. Also, they measure retention and attrition after only one year of teaching.

The Odell and Ferraro study is notable for the fact that they collected information on mentored beginners after 4 years of teaching. They tracked down information on two cohorts of teachers in New Mexico, managing to locate 141 of the original 160 teachers (88%) four years later, 96% of whom were still in the classroom. Under the conservative assumption that the unlocated individuals were no longer teaching, the percentage retained is reduced to a still very high 84%. The teachers completed questionnaires, from which Odell and Ferraro determined that, in retrospect, during their first year of teaching the beginners most valued the emotional support they had received from their mentors. They had no control group, but quoted, as a comparison, state attrition rates of 9% per year for nonmentored teachers, resulting in a 4-year retention rate of 64%. We have no demographic information on the school districts, no idea what attrition they had experienced before the mentoring program was introduced, and the authors do not report how they selected the districts for study in the first place.[122]

The last two studies are contained in two reports on the Texas Beginning Teacher Support System (TxBESS), a statewide program to assist new teachers similar to California's Beginning Teacher Support and Assessment (BTSA) program.[123] We learn from Ed Fuller and the State Board for Educator Certification (SBEC)website that 89.2% of Tx-BESS teachers returned after one year, and 84.4% after 2 years, compared with 80.8% and 75.4% for non-TxBESS teachers (Ingersoll and Kralik quote slightly different numbers). The differences are statistically significant, comparing those who were retained in Texas public schools with those who disappeared from the payroll, some of whom may have left the state but remained in teaching. Unfortunately, the authors did not monitor the variation in program features across the state, although the effects were found across schools of all demographic types and for both certified and uncertified teachers. It is quite possible that programs ran the gamut of Smith and Ingersoll's different levels of support, including some that may have had no mentoring at all.

Libby Grant conducted a meta-analysis of research on induction and mentoring and retention for her doctoral dissertation.[124] The author's data reduction criteria resulted in nine primary studies from California, Texas, Montana, North Dakota, Illinois, Georgia, and Maryland. She concluded that the induction and mentoring programs had a statistically significant effect on teacher retention, as did the quality of the program and its location. Retention was related to whether states funded induction programs and whether the program was partnered with a university.

If we were to limit ourselves by the strict parameters for the inclusion of studies in the manner of these researchers, there would be nothing else to review. However, a small number of other studies, some of which are mentioned in passing by these authors, are worthy of further inspection. Over recent years, the California BTSA program has collected retention data from across the state. Each year the California Commission on Teacher Credentialing (CCTC) asks BTSA programs to submit their data on teacher retention. In a preliminary report on these data issued early in this century, the Commission examined employment data on its teachers over 4 years in order to determine how many left the public school system and when.[125] These results were then compared to Ingersoll's national data. The Commission determined that 84% of the 1995–96 new teachers were still in the system after 4 years, compared to the national retention rate of 67%. Relying on payroll data alone, the Commission may have included individuals not in the classroom but employed elsewhere in the public school system. Likewise, some of those reported lost to teaching may have taken positions in private schools or in other states. Also, we cannot know the effects of any particular package of induction support in the manner of those identified by Ingersoll, since BTSA programs vary widely in their degree of comprehensiveness. The Commission's 2002 publication promises that a follow-up report on the dynamics of teacher turnover would be available in 2003, but at the time of writing, there is no indication of the existence of such a report.

A study of new teacher retention comparing supported and unsupported new teachers in one of the California BTSA regions (incorporating Riverside, Inyo, Mono, and San Bernadino counties) reported lower retention rates.[126] After two years 77.6% of BTSA and 46.3% of non-BTSA teachers were still in teaching in this BTSA region. The percentages of employed teachers may be underestimated, however, since the California Basic Educational Data System (CBEDS), the source of data for this study, does not collect information on teachers outside their catchment areas. Also, this study has not been published following a presentation at the 1999 annual meeting of the American Educational Research Association. For this reason, it will not be often cited in the literature. A companion study conducted one year later reported that 89% of the new teachers from the same program were still teaching the following year. As with the state data, these numbers do not distinguish among attrition, turnover, movers, and leavers, and they do not take into account any school conditions that may interact with the existence or type of BTSA program. These issues notwithstanding, the data suggest that new teachers who receive induction support are less likely to move or leave than those who do not.[127]

In 2001 a colleague and I conducted a study that was not included in Ingersoll and Kralik's review because the comparison group consisted of teachers with a less comprehensive mentoring support than the treatment group rather than no support at all.[128] Our study followed up on 72 teachers who had been enrolled in a comprehensive induction program (falling under Smith and Ingersoll's highest level of support) 6 years earlier. We were able to locate all but three of them in order to determine their current status, and, in most cases, their work histories. Assuming the unlocated individuals had left the profession, 88% were still teaching (or on temporary leave), and a further 6% held some other position in education. We interviewed 58 of the teachers and found that 38% had remained in the same school for the 6-year period, 47% in the same district, and 71% in the same state. These overall retention numbers are higher than national and state averages reported in the California state study.[129] Our comparison group consisted of teachers who had started in the same school year, but in neighboring districts outside the service area, where they may have received some induction support, or none at all. They were, however, harder to locate, and we were able to find only 20 of the 46 teachers from the lists that came from the district office. Eleven of the 20, or 55%, were still classroom teachers. Since those still teaching were likely to be easier to track down than those who had moved away or on to other careers, this estimate of retention is probably high. Our study was unusual in that it looked at retention after 6 years. Most studies only track retention over one or two years. We conducted a follow-up study with a more recent and larger cohort from the same comprehensive program and found identical retention rates across a similar time span.

In a report published by the Public Policy Institute of California, Deborah Reed and colleagues looked at, among other things, the influence of California's BTSA program on teacher retention rates in California.[130] They combined data from the California Council on Teacher Credentialing with data from the California Employment Development Department in order to track teachers over the 10-year period from 1990 to 2000. Looking from a state and district level, they found that districts that adopted BTSA programs during the early 1990s improved retention by 26% for teachers with multiple-subject certifications and by 16% for teachers with single-subject credentials. There are some limitations to their data, including the fact that new teachers were defined as new-to-California rather than new-to-teaching, and so they counted among that group experienced teachers who transferred from other states. Also, by defining teachers as those possessing a credential, they included in the sample educators who may have been in other educational positions such as school administration.

Peter Youngs examined the Connecticut BEST program in a report prepared for NCTAF.[131] As we saw in Chapter 2, the BEST program provides new teachers with mentoring and other support, including free in-service training courses relating to teaching methods and expertise. During their first year, new teachers work with mentors or other support persons, one of whom must have gone through the BEST training. This is roughly equivalent to Smith and Ingersoll's category of "induction plus collaboration." Youngs found that attrition and migration were much lower among BEST teachers than for those of similar socioeconomic backgrounds in nontreatment districts. It is possible, however, that better working conditions such as higher teacher salaries and strong instructional leadership in the target districts may have combined with the mentoring program to produce higher retention rates.

In her doctoral dissertation Carolyn Elmore compared the effects of two kinds of mentoring on new teacher effectiveness and retention in two Maryland programs.[132] One program provided full-time mentor teacher consultants (MTCs) who were placed to assist first-year teachers in three schools selected because of low test scores and high turnover. A second program offered peer mentors (PMs) a small stipend with no release time to assist new teachers in the remaining 23 schools in the county. Two years later, teacher retention in the MTC schools had improved while the PM schools continued to lose teachers. On the other hand, teacher effectiveness ratings were better for the teachers in the PM group.

Jonah Rockoff conducted a study of new teachers in New York City who had received a modified version of the Santa Cruz NTC model of teacher induction.[133] He reports some evidence that mentoring affects whether a teacher completes the school year, and there was an indication that having a mentor who previously worked in the same school as a mentor or teacher has an impact on whether a teacher decides to remain in the school the following year. This, he suggests, points to the importance for a mentor to school-specific knowledge. There are some limitations to this study, not the smallest of which is the fact that data were only available for 2 years, and that the program was only offered to first-year teachers. The Santa Cruz model underscores the importance of having induction support last for 2 years, as the second year is when there is opportunity to focus more on instructional issues. This is most important when considering effects on teaching practice and student achievement, a point to which I will return later in the book.

In 2005 Kavita Kapadia and her colleagues surveyed 1,737 novice teachers in Chicago Public Schools.[134] They determined levels of induction and mentoring support, dividing them into three groups: weak, average, and strong. About one fifth of these teachers report that they were not involved in any induction program, even though it was a requirement. The researchers did not look at actual retention or turnover data, but measured the influence of participation in induction programs on three outcomes: the novice teachers' teaching experiences, their intentions to stay in teaching, and their intentions to stay in the same school. They found that, when adjusting for school context, participation in an induction program, by itself, had little effect on the three outcomes. However, the teachers in the strong induction group showed higher levels on all three outcomes. Mentoring was an important component, especially at the elementary level, but the comprehensive induction supports from all sources had the most effect on intentions to remain in the same school. Kapadia and colleagues conclude that programs should focus on selection and training of mentors to ensure they give high levels of support, and that teacher collaboration and principal assistance are the most influential factors for novices.

These studies and reviews suggest that mentoring is correlated with the retention of new teachers in the profession, and may also be related to decreased turnover from district to district and school to school. The clearest implication, however, is that most studies have limitations that are liable to compromise any conclusions one is able to draw from them. Either they do not specify the level of mentoring or the nature of the induction program under investigation, or, more likely, they combine results from a range of different programs. Furthermore, many do not have comparison data, and none is set up with a true control group. Of those that compare different kinds of programs, it appears that comprehensive support that has the enhanced "packages" of components described by Smith and Ingersoll are more likely to have an effect on turnover than basic mentoring programs. Most other published work on the relation between induction/mentoring and retention is either purely qualitative in nature or has a theoretical or policy perspective.

ASSESSING THE EVIDENCE: IS TEACHER INDUCTION EFFECTIVE IN REDUCING TEACHER ATTRITION?

Anyone reading this chapter should have already reached the conclusion that there is no obvious answer to this question. First, there is no accepted set of definitions for the phenomena of retention, turnover, and attrition. Thus statistics on teacher movement vary across different studies, partly according to the definitions employed. Second, there is disagreement about the proportion of teachers who are actually lost to the profession. For example, when researchers take into account the numbers of (predominantly female) teachers who quit temporarily in order to start or raise a family and return a year or two later, the inclusion of their numbers under the attrition column results in an overestimate of teacher loss. Other studies fail to account for teachers who move to a different state, or they include as beginning teachers those who are merely new to the district, not to the profession. It appears one can acknowledge, however, that more teachers leave the classroom than is desirable, and that more of them do so in their early years. There is also evidence that teachers tend to take early retirement more often than members of other professions, such as nurses and social workers, thus creating the previously mentioned U-shaped curve.

Given that one is forced to work with these somewhat messy data, is it possible to determine any correlation between teacher induction and teacher retention? There is no shortage of attempts to measure this connection, but most look only at single programs (which themselves vary in the components they offer) and have no comparison data from teachers without a program. Moreover, many do not actually measure retention, but rather poll the teachers' intentions to stay or leave. Consequently, these studies produce findings that are not reliable or generalizable. The best multivariate research, which uses large survey databases such as the SASS/TFS, suffers from being able to measure retention over one year only, and must rely on rough agglomerations of program components based on teachers' self-reports to produce a description of the kinds of induction support that the novice teachers putatively receive. Nevertheless, because the data set is so large, the evidence points strongly to the conclusion that the more components of induction support teachers report having received, regardless of their actual content and level of implementation, the greater the likelihood that they will remain in teaching.

There are additional problems with the research that concerns teachers who leave. No study has data on who quits because they are unable to withstand the challenges of teaching; few studies factor into their equations the percentage of attrition that is desirable or whether more or less effective teachers are leaving; and most studies, while recognizing that some teachers leave for personal reasons, fail to distinguish that group when measuring attrition and correlating it with induction support. Finally, a large number of teachers move from school to school and district to district, or change educational roles, often because of economic factors or issues related to working conditions. From the school's and the students' perspectives these transfers have the same repercussions as when a teacher quits the profession. Induction may play a role in reducing this kind of turnover, but it is difficult to measure, and its influence is hard to distinguish from the effects of increases in salary or improvements in other working conditions.

At most, the research indicates that induction support is positively correlated with retention. Because of the exigencies described above and the other contextual variables that are likely to covary with the amount and kind of induction support any teacher receives in a particular setting, one must reserve judgment about the existence and likely strength of any postulated causal relationship.

Chapter 4

Induction Programs and the Development of Teaching Practice

THE IMPORTANCE OF TEACHER QUALITY

Since the No Child Left Behind Act (NCLB) was passed in 2002, the term *teacher quality* has been close to the surface of everyone's consciousness. It is now fairly well documented that the best school predictor of student outcomes is high-quality, effective teaching as defined by performance in the classroom.[1] Therefore, before looking at the issue of relating induction to changes in teaching practice (and, by implication, in teacher quality) I will briefly review some of the research on teacher quality and teacher effectiveness, whose findings are by no means straightforward and whose interpretations often depend on the ideology of the researchers.[2]

As far back as 1966 educators learned from the Coleman report that student characteristics, particularly socioeconomic background, accounted for a far greater proportion of differences in student performance than did school factors. Of the school factors that could be manipulated, teacher quality accounted for more of the differences in student test scores than all others (excepting student components).[3] The Coleman report focused on teacher characteristics such as years of experience, degrees obtained, and test performance, all of which could be easily quantified. Subsequent research, with the benefit of value-added modeling (VAM),[4] has shown that these characteristics account for only a small percentage of what makes a teacher effective in the classroom.[5] In addition, when they do correlate, it is within specific contexts: For example, a masters degree is more likely to be related to the effective teaching of math and science.[6] Dan Goldhaber found that only 3% of a teacher's contribution to student learning was associated with factors such as years of experience and degrees obtained, while the remaining 97% was associated with "qualities and behaviors that could not be isolated and identified."[7] Experience seems to make a difference in the early years of a teacher's career. During the first four or five years, teachers appear to gain in effectiveness in terms of improving student achievement scores, but they level off, indicating that years of experience beyond the fifth year contribute little or no additional benefit to student achievement. This may, in part, reflect the graduation and labor market conditions that prevailed at the time of the teacher's initial hiring, and experienced teachers may make other contributions to their schools, for example as coaches and mentors to less experienced colleagues.

Another characteristic of recent interest is the level of a teacher's teaching skills, often referred to as pedagogical knowledge. In the absence of any direct measure, pedagogical knowledge is usually operationalized as performance on licensure exams or the kind of licensure obtained.[8] One early study reviewed performance on the National Teacher Exam (NTE),[9] and found that district averages of teachers on this test correlated with student achievement.[10] The problem is that scores on the NTE conflated teaching skills and subject-matter knowledge. Recently, Doug Harris and Tim Sass used sophisticated statistical techniques to control for inadequate measures of teacher training and difficulties addressing the nonrandom selection of teachers to students and of teachers to training, and found no evidence that teachers with higher college entrance exam scores or who receive undergraduate degrees in the subject they teach are more effective than other teachers.[11]

Jennifer King Rice focused on five teacher attributes: experience, preparation programs and degrees, certification, coursework, and teacher test scores. Recognizing that evidence is not always available to enable us to reject the existence of some of these connections, she concludes that some of the more refined measures of what teachers know and can do, such as subject-specific credentials and special coursework, are better predictors of student learning than variables such as degrees and total number of course credits.[12]

Linda Darling-Hammond analyzed state-level data from California and concluded that the state proportion of well-qualified teachers (i.e., those with full certification and subject-related major) was the best predictor of achievement in reading and math.[13] As Dan Goldhaber points out, Darling-Hammond's study suffers from its reliance on state aggregated achievement data, which are open to the influence of many uncontrollable and unidentifiable variables. Goldhaber and his colleague Dominic Brewer overcame this problem by examining the issue at the teacher level. They concluded that teachers with standard certification outperformed those with no certification, but were indistinguishable from teachers with emergency credentials.[14] State differences in licensure requirements may account for some of these differences. Other studies have found no differences in effectiveness between regularly certified teachers and those who took alternative paths to certification.[15]

The research is clear that having a good teacher is important, but undecided as to what makes for a good teacher. A high-quality teacher may have considerable impact on student learning. For example, Eric Hanushek found that, all things being equal, a student with a very high quality teacher will achieve a learning gain of 1.5 grade-level equivalents, while a student with a low-quality teacher achieves a gain of only 0.5 grade-level equivalents.[16] This translates to one year's growth being attributable to teacher quality differences. More recently Daniel Aaronson and colleagues examined data from the Chicago Public Schools and found that a one standard deviation, one semester improvement in math teacher quality raises student math scores by 0.13 grade equivalents or, over one year, roughly one fifth of average yearly gains.[17] Another study of data from Texas schools found that little of the variation in teacher quality was explained by observable characteristics such as education or experience. The authors of the study concluded that the effects of reducing class size by 10 students (a costly undertaking) are smaller than the benefit of moving one standard deviation up the teacher quality distribution, thus highlighting the importance of teacher effectiveness in the determination of school quality.[18]

William Sanders, who pioneered the Tennessee Value-Added Assessment System, in summarizing his own studies stated that especially in math the cumulative and residual effects of teachers are still measurable at least 4 years after students leave a classroom.[19] A study by Barbara Nye and colleagues, unusual because it randomly assigned students to classes, estimated teacher effects on student achievement over 4 years. Their estimates of teacher effects on achievement gains were similar in magnitude to those of previous studies done by economists, but they found larger effects on mathematics than on reading achievement.[20]

In spite of such findings, it is unfortunate that years of educational research have left us barely wiser about which aspects of teacher behavior are related to student learning. The following statement from a recent paper by Dan Goldhaber and Emily Anthony sums up the situation well:

Education research has failed to reach a consensus over which, if any, readily identifiable teacher characteristics are associated with students' learning gains, and it remains an open question as to whether it is even possible to judge teachers' effectiveness using measures other than direct observations of their teaching.[21]

Goldhaber and Anthony do not go into detail about how such direct observations might best be conducted. In the past, classroom observation checklists that score whether a teacher shows a certain set of behaviors, have done so frequently without judging whether they are appropriate in the specific situation. In other words, they ignore contextual factors related to the school, students, the time in the academic year, the state of the curriculum, the availability of resources, and so on. In addition, by focusing exclusively on classroom performance, much evidence about teaching is inevitably left out.[22] Because of the high stakes attributed to test scores, most observation systems for teacher evaluation have been more concerned with the reliability and the objectivity of the scores they produce than with their validity.[23] I will explore these and other issues later in this chapter.

In spite of recognized challenges in evaluating teaching, if we agree that teacher quality is likely to be better demonstrated by classroom performance than by any of the quantifiable attributes such as degree, kind of certification, or even years of experience, then the part that a good induction program might play in teacher development is potentially of great importance. Certainly, a desired outcome of induction support for new teachers is that their teaching practice improve to a greater extent than if they were left to their own devices. It follows that, in order to be able to measure whether any improvement in practice is taking place, we have to know two things: what to look for, and how to measure it.

WHAT TO LOOK FOR

In a wonderful article in the *Teachers College Record*, Gary Fenstermacher and Virginia Richardson analyze the concept of quality in teaching.[24] The article starts with the following pithy questions that are fundamental to our pursuit of information about the possible influence of induction support on teaching practice: "What is good teaching? Would we recognize it if we saw it?" They draw attention to the important distinction between *good teaching* (the worthiness of the activity) and *successful teaching* (the realization of intended outcomes), then go on to make the point that *quality teaching* encompasses both good and successful teaching. They review how quality teaching is instantiated in research from three perspectives: process-product,[25] cognitive science, and constructivism.[26] They conclude that an assessment of quality teaching requires that, in addition to focusing on the teacher, one take into account contextual factors such as the state of the learners, the character of the social surroundings, and the availability and extent of opportunity to teach and learn. Thus the nature of teacher quality is elusive and contested, yet not without those who profess to know how to evaluate it:

> [This] has not stopped others from asserting that they know quality teaching when they see it, they know how to determine whether it is occurring or not, and they know this across schools, districts, states, and nations. Many such claims lack not only a good understanding of teaching but also a humility for the challenge of appraising anything so complex as the nature and consequences of human relationships, particularly between adults and children in the otherwise unworldly setting of the schools of the early 21st century.[27]

If we agree with Fenstermacher and Richardson that quality in teaching embraces the two concepts of good and successful, then we should quickly recognize that most existing measures rely on the one but not the other. In other words, teachers tend to be evaluated either through some kind of classroom observation protocol (to measure good teaching, however defined) or, less frequently, by their demonstrated ability to raise student test scores (to determine successful teaching). Classroom observation measures tend to be based on some set of norms of good teaching, such as those identified in state or national standards,[28] but these are rarely grounded in evidence of any *empirical* connection to successful teaching as embodied in student learning, although they do examine teaching in the light of student learning.[29]

This brings me back to the question: What do we look for? For the purpose of exploring changes in teacher behaviors that may be related to induction support, either from a mentor or another kind of professional development, we would want to check for elements of good teaching practice that have been the focus of the induction program or are most likely to be influenced by it and preferably are observable in the classroom. Assuming we are able to define those elements, we must then decide on the size of the sample of teaching we need to observe in order to feel confident that we can characterize a teacher's level of practice in the chosen areas. This may be part of a lesson, a complete lesson, several lessons, a curriculum unit, or several units. Having made that decision, we need to determine when to conduct the observations. We may decide to observe toward the end of spring to capture the cumulative effects of a school year of induction support, or at both the beginning and end of the academic year to measure any change. A third alternative would be to observe at intervals throughout the year in the hope of seeing changes as they occur. Both purpose and available resources will determine which choice is made, and the resulting data will vary accordingly.

WHAT OTHERS HAVE LOOKED FOR

From the long history of research on teaching, we can identify three broad domains of teaching activities or tasks that have been the object of inquiry: (1) those that concern planning for teaching and understanding the subject matter; (2) those that deal with the interactive task of teaching including the monitoring and evaluation of student learning; and (3) those involving reflection, continuing education, and interaction with colleagues.[30] These domains have been described, respectively, as "preactive," "interactive," and "postactive."[31] While a teacher may address tasks in any of these domains at any time, I focus here on those that can be determined from observing a teacher in the classroom, those normally described as interactive. The so-called process-product studies in the 1970s and 1980s focused on teacher behavior and on how teacher behaviors related to outcomes in student learning, usually represented by student achievement scores in math and reading.[32] However, during the past 15–20 years new conceptions of teaching have emerged, and these have implications for how researchers assess and evaluate teaching. Studies on teacher thinking (how teachers make sense of their students and classroom events and how their understandings influence the decisions they make), teacher development (how teachers grow and develop over their careers and the factors that affect their growth), teacher learning (constructivist perspectives on the process through which teachers learn to teach and how that process may be facilitated), and teacher knowledge (the sort of knowledge teachers need in order to teach well) have fundamentally changed how teaching is viewed and what it takes to teach. A review of the findings from the literature on teaching practice in general is beyond the scope of this book, so I will move directly into an examination of how teaching practice is measured.

WAYS OF MEASURING TEACHING PRACTICE

The only reliable way to measure the nature and quality of teaching practice is through classroom observation. This doesn't mean that researchers have not used the alternative method of surveying or interviewing teachers in order to collect self-report information about their teaching behavior, their feelings about teaching, or their feelings about their ability to teach. Using teacher self-report data as a proxy for observations of practice is more practical in that it takes less time and fewer resources, but it is, for obvious reasons, less reliable.

I will return to the self-report literature, but for now I devote my attention to classroom observation as a means of gathering data on teaching practice. There are various methods for collecting observational data. First, one may simply watch a lesson and take descriptive accounts in the form of field notes, with or without a checklist of things to watch for. Second, one could use a holistic rating, whereby an expert would observe a teacher and make a judgment as to whether the person was performing at, for example, a basic, proficient, or advanced level. A third option would be to use some existing observation instrument, of which there are many. A fourth possibility would be to create a new instrument.

Descriptive accounts tend to be selective, inconsistent, full of interpretation, and often not comparable to other records of classroom events. Holistic ratings are purely subjective. That leaves formal observation instruments, which can be unreliable if they require a lot of training or interpretation. It would take up far too much space to review the multitude of observation instruments that have been developed over the years. Anita Simon and Gil Boyer anthologized 99 such instruments that existed up to 1974 during the heyday of classroom observation.[33] Following a decline of interest in observation of teaching during the 1980s, Carolyn Lavely and her colleagues reviewed instruments that were contemporary in 1994, during a resurgence that, they claimed, was prompted in part by the accountability and teacher minimum competency movements.[34] Traditionally, observation instruments have been categorized as either low or high inference. A *low inference measure* is a rating system that classifies specific, denotable, relatively objective classroom behavior and is recorded as frequency counts by an observer. A *high inference measure* is a rating system that requires an observer to make an inference from a series of classroom events using specific constructs, such as satisfaction, cohesiveness, cultural sensitivity, and so on.

A classic example of a low inference observation instrument is the Interaction Analysis System (IAS) developed by Ned Flanders.[35] The IAS was used extensively throughout the 1960s and 1970s in its original form as well as in modified forms,[36] and it was also customized for bilingual interaction analysis.[37] This analysis system and many other low-inference behavioral measures prevalent throughout the 1960s had an impact on how to describe teacher and class behavior through observations of the way teacher and students interacted. The following list displays the categories of the IAS:

Teacher Talk: Indirect Influence

1. *Accepting feelings:* Accepting and clarifying the feeling tone of the students in a nonthreatening manner. Feelings may be positive or negative. Predicting or recalling feelings is included.
2. *Praising or encouraging:* Praising or encouraging student action or behavior. Jokes that release tension (not at the expense of another individual), nodding head, or saying, "Um hum?" or "Go on" are included.
3. *Accepting or using ideas of student:* Clarifying, building, or developing ideas suggested by a student. As teacher brings more of his own ideas into play, this shifts to Category 5.
4. *Asking questions:* Asking a question about content or procedure with the intent that a student answer.

Teacher Talk: Direct influence

5. *Lecturing:* Giving facts or opinions about content or procedure; expressing own ideas, asking rhetorical questions.
6. *Giving ideas:* Directions, commands, or orders to which a student is expected to comply.
7. *Criticizing or justifying authority:* Statements intended to change student behavior from nonacceptable to acceptable pattern; bawling someone out; stating why the teacher is doing what he is doing; extreme self-reference.

Student Talk

8. *Student talk-response:* Talk by students in response to teacher. Teacher initiates the contact or solicits student statement.
9. *Student talk-initiation:* Talk by students that they initiate. If calling on student is only to indicate who may talk next, ob-

server must decide whether student wanted to talk. If so, use this category.
10. *Silence or confusion:* Pauses, short periods of silence, and periods of confusion in which communications cannot be understood by the observer.

Another low-inference instrument is the *Observation Schedule and Record* (OScAR), which the authors describe as a method for observing and recording classroom behavior.[38] The OScAR has 14 scoring keys:

1. Time spent on reading
2. Problem-structuring teacher statements
3. Autonomous administrative groupings
4. Pupil leadership activities
5. Freedom of movement
6. Manifest teacher hostility
7. Supportive teacher behavior
8. Time spent on social studies
9. Disorderly pupil behavior
10. Verbal activities
11. Traditional pupil activities
12. Teacher's verbal output
13. Audiovisual materials
14. Autonomous social groupings

These keys can be categorized into three scales:

1. Emotional climate
2. Verbal emphasis
3. Social organization

The authors had high hopes for their instrument, and saw the OScAR as an important means to help solve practical problems such as how to select students likely to become successful teachers, how to screen out those who cannot get along with children, and what ought to be the content of teacher training. Surprisingly, they found that the effect of the emotional climate scale overshadowed the other two scales of the OScAR.

The IAS and many other low-inference measures reflecting the behaviorist perspective prevalent throughout the 1960s had a widespread impact on how to describe teacher and class behavior. However, they were not connected to any established teaching standards, so research studies explored connections between styles of teacher-student interaction and student learning outcomes. Subsequent research has included the use of high-inference ratings as well as such methods as teacher interviews and narrative recordings, but instruments using low-inference coding procedures are more prominent in the published literature, because they are more likely to demonstrate a strong connection with student outcomes.

For comparison purposes, I include two examples of high-inference measures. The first was developed by Charles Teddlie and colleagues as part of a program of research to study effective schools.[39] The Classroom Observation Instrument (COI) was developed to allow researchers to record information on a variety of behaviors that the authors "generally considered to constitute effective teaching."[40] In developing this open-ended instrument the authors reviewed several articles that summarized proven characteristics of effective teaching, using in particular, the work of Barak Rosenshine to create 14 indicators of their own. Rosenshine had developed a list of six instructional functions that were commonly identified as necessary for effective teaching:

1. Review, checking previous day's work (and re-teaching if necessary)
2. Presenting new content/skills
3. Initial student practice (and checking for understanding)
4. Feedback and correctives (and re-teaching if necessary)
5. Student independent practice
6. Weekly and monthly reviews[41]

The COI allowed the researchers to complete qualitative field notes on how teachers addressed each of the instructional functions identified by Rosenshine. These qualitative field notes were used as the basis for case studies that would verify and expand on more readily quantified data including achievement test scores.

Another high-influence measure, developed by Deborah Saldana and Hersh Waxman, was the Multicultural Teaching Observation Instrument (MTOI), which was used to assess types and amounts of multicultural teaching that occurred in classrooms that included a mix of African American, White, and Hispanic students.[42] The MTOI consists of 18 indicators or items that are grouped into the three categories of teacher support, equity, and integration of culture:

Teacher Support of Students

Teacher respects all students.
Teacher treats students as individuals.
Teacher is willing to help each student.
Teacher is patient when students have trouble understanding.
Teacher relates to students in a culturally acceptable manner.
Teacher is sensitive to students' culture.

Classroom Equity

Students from different ethnic groups are grouped together.
Students from different ethnic groups appear to work well together.
Teacher works to reduce inequities in the classroom.
Teacher has several "favorite" students in class.
Teacher fosters gender-related stereotypes.
Teacher dislikes several students.

Integration of Students' Culture

Teacher uses culturally appropriate material.
Pictures of diverse cultural groups are displayed.
Pictures of students/families are displayed.
Teacher elicits information from students about their culture.
Teacher uses examples of other cultures when explaining or demonstrating concepts/ideas.
There are books about American ethnic groups in the classroom.

The MTOI is completed after the observation of a single lesson, and may be performed at different times to record changes in teacher behavior. The items were validated by five professors who taught multicultural education and five teachers from urban schools. Even more so than the IAS or OScAR, the MTOI is developed around a set of categories that are similar to teaching standards. In other words, the categories of teacher support, equity, and integration of culture may be thought of as standards against which to be judged, whereas the categories in the IAS, OScAR, and the COI include elements that are more descriptive and less value-laden.

With the trend toward accountability, accelerated by NCLB, there is now more emphasis on teaching standards, and some states have developed evaluation systems whereby districts may be held accountable for teacher effectiveness. This has given rise to a number of teacher evaluation instruments that are both summative and formative. That is to say, they fulfill dual use as measures both of accountability and professional development.[43]

Instead of comparing teachers to one another, these systems weigh multiple forms of evidence on teacher performance against a set of detailed rating scales based on the standards that describe several levels of teacher performance. The rating scales—typically called *rubrics*—provide guidance to evaluators in making judgments, lessen subjectivity, and offer a common criterion reference for ratings. The standards and rubrics also afford guidance to teachers on what behaviors and skills are expected. The standards are broad descriptions of what teachers need to know and be able to do, and they are based on the recognition that there are many ways in which teachers can meet these standards. As such, they differ from standards formulated in early competence-based assessment that indicate prescribed behaviors. Standards are developed through consultation with experienced teachers and teacher educators. Some assessment systems are subject and level specific, whereas others may be used in all subject areas and at all grade levels. They all rely on "authentic" assessments of teacher competence.

From the evidence gathered from performances on these authentic assessments, assessors make judgments about whether an individual meets the criteria specified in the standards. Standards-based evaluation systems typically require both a more extensive collection of evidence about teachers' practices, including frequent observations of classroom behavior, and a review of artifacts such as lesson plans and samples of student work. They also require more extensive rater training to develop a common framework for applying the standards.

A widely used example of such a teacher evaluation system is the *Framework for Teaching* developed by Charlotte Danielson in 1996 and revised in 2007.[44] According to Danielson, the *Framework for Teaching* is based on a review and synthesis of the empirical and theoretical research on what teachers should know and be able to do in the classroom. Adopting a constructivist approach to teaching, the *Framework for Teaching* assumes that instructional decisions by teachers are purposeful and teaching activities and assignments are chosen because they serve instructional goals. It includes standards that focus on behavioral responsibilities and competencies rather than specific content or subject matter knowledge, though the transfer of that knowledge is an important activity embedded within the Framework for Teaching.

The Framework for Teaching is constructed around four teaching domains. Twenty-two specific components are contained within the four domains:

Domain 1: Planning and Preparation Components
Domain 2: The Classroom Environment Components
Domain 3: Instruction Components
Domain 4: Professional Responsibilities Components

Each component, in turn, is broken down into more specific behavioral elements. Each element has four levels of performance: unsatisfactory, basic, proficient, and distinguished. Rubrics for each behavioral element provide standards of performance for each of the four performance levels. As an example, the following rubric contains the performance standards for "The Teacher Interaction with Students" and "Student Interaction" elements included within the components of Domain 2:

- *Unsatisfactory:* Teacher interaction with at least some students is negative, demeaning, sarcastic, or inappropriate to the age or culture of the students. Students exhibit disrespect for teacher. Student interactions are characterized by conflict, sarcasm, or put-downs.
- *Basic:* Teacher-student interactions are generally appropriate but may reflect occasional inconsistencies, favoritism, or disregard for students' cultures. Students exhibit only minimal respect for teacher. Students do not demonstrate negative behavior toward one another.
- *Proficient:* Teacher-student interactions are friendly and demonstrate general warmth, caring, and respect. Such interactions are appropriate to developmental and cultural norms. Students exhibit respect for teacher. Student interactions are generally polite and respectful.
- *Distinguished:* Teacher demonstrates genuine caring and respect for individual students. Students exhibit respect for teacher as an individual, beyond that for the role. Students demonstrate genuine caring for one another as individuals and as students.[45]

It is important to note that the *Framework for Teaching* seeks to provide a comprehensive assessment of teaching practice, yet be general enough to apply to all subject areas and grade levels. It is a generalized depiction of teaching activities that must be assessed by considering the individual context of the teacher and classroom. Numerous school districts throughout the country have developed and implemented teacher performance evaluation systems based on modified versions of Danielson's *Framework*, where classroom observations may be just one of several sources of information for the assessment. Even though the rubrics are extensively laid out, there is no doubt that this evaluation system falls into the high-inference category.

Several researchers have conducted multilevel studies in different settings to test whether teachers with high evaluation scores on the Danielson *Framework*, or a modified version of it, also have classes with correspondingly high student achievement gains.[46] All of these studies, using Hierarchical Linear Modeling (HLM)[47] techniques, documented that teachers with higher evaluation scores produced slightly larger learning gains in student achievement as measured by standardized tests. It must be stressed that standards-based assessments such as the *Framework* involve more than classroom observation to arrive at its evaluation for a particular teacher. A full assessment across the four domains as described by Danielson requires, in addition to frequent observations of classroom practice, the use of artifacts such as lesson plans and samples of student work in order to provide a rich, intensive picture of teacher performance.

In spite of these many years of effort by researchers to construct instruments for evaluating teaching, they are not thought of very highly as measures of accountability, for the most part because they are perceived as having low validity. Kenneth Peterson had the following to say about teacher evaluations, which in most settings are conducted by school principals:

> At the same time that its development has been neglected, teacher evaluation is a widespread activity in the schools. In this activity, where good practice should be common, inadequate efforts and materials are the order of the day. Poor practice in teacher evaluation is quietly accepted, according to teachers, administrators, and researchers. Evaluations look about the same in district after district, and for teacher after teacher. When there are problems with bad teachers or bad evaluations, people talk about it like few other educational problems; the rest of the time teacher evaluation is ignored or disparaged.[48]

There is not much evidence to suggest a strong relationship between teacher evaluation ratings and student academic outcomes. Many studies across the years report quite small correlations between principal evaluations and student achievement. In 1987 Donald Medley and Homer Coker summarized the research up to that point this way:

> To this day, almost all educational personnel decisions are based on judgments which, according to the research, are only slightly more accurate than they would be if they were based on pure chance.[49]

Medley and Coker suggested that the studies they reviewed suffered from (1) problems related to aggregation of principal ratings across schools (thereby opening up contamination of school effects), and (2) statistical analyses that involved violated assumptions across different classes, and averaging class gains with adjustments, thus resulting in an exaggeration rather than a reduction of the differences. In their own study they focused on the accuracy of principals' judgments of teacher performance instead of the validity of principals' ratings. However, they, too, found that the accuracy of principals' judgments was low.[50]

Brian Jacob and Lars Lefgren criticized these and some more recent research studies[51] for being generally based on small, nonrepresentative samples, not accounting adequately for measurement error, and relying on objective measures of teacher performance that are likely biased.[52] In their own work, they conducted an analysis that compared principal evaluations of teacher effectiveness against levels of teacher education and experience, as well as effectiveness based on student achievement gains. An interesting contribution of their study is their deliberation on the sources of information that principals use in making judgments about teacher effectiveness. These include, in addition to formal and informal classroom observations, reports from parents and student achievement scores. They point out that principals will differ in the degree of their sophistication in accessing data and in their interpretation of any signals they receive, and that these differences may be reflected in their ultimate judgments of the teachers' effectiveness. For the purposes of our focus on the possible effects of induction on teacher practice and our estimation of that practice through classroom observation, we should be cognizant of the fact that we would not be taking into account any of these other data sources. It is not unreasonable to assume that principals who rely exclusively on classroom observation data (say for beginning teachers or teachers new to their school) are likely to be even less accurate in their evaluations than those who have access to other sources of information.

EVIDENCE FROM PSYCHOLOGY AND COGNITIVE SCIENCE
ABOUT JUDGMENTS OF HUMAN BEHAVIOR

Given what we know from the educational research literature about the evaluation of teaching through classroom observation, we have no reason to be confident that any judgments about teaching practice are likely to be highly correlated with increases in student achievement, even if we are able to select an instrument that is appropriate for our purpose, and even if we are convinced that we have access to an acceptable sample of teaching behavior.

Added to this, educational researchers do not take into account what is known about judgments of human behavior from the fields of psychology and cognitive science when they are considering the accuracy of evaluations that are based solely on observations of teaching behavior. There are several challenges that the psychological and cognitive science research presents.

Take, for example, the phenomenon of *confirmation bias*. This describes a tendency to seek, embellish, and emphasize experiences that support rather than challenge already held beliefs. As an information processor, it filters experiences in a confirmatory manner, highlighting those that are consistent with its conceptual biases and ignoring or discrediting those that are not. A classic study conducted by the late British psychologist Peter Wason[53] was one of the earliest demonstrations of a notion that had been described back in the seventeenth century by Sir Francis Bacon, the English philosopher and essayist.[54]

Wason presented undergraduate subjects with a triplet of numbers (2, 4, 6) and told them that these numbers conformed to a simple relational rule. Their task was to discover this relational rule by generating other triplets of numbers and checking with the experimenter to see if their triplet conformed to the rule. Subjects were told to announce a hypothesis about the rule only when they were very confident that it was correct. If it was incorrect, they were so informed and asked to continue searching for the correct answer. While the actual rule was simply "any ascending sequence," the subjects seemed to have a great deal of difficulty in inducing it, often announcing rules that were far more complex than the correct rule. The subjects seemed to test only "positive" examples—triplets that subjects believed would conform to their rule and confirm their hypothesis. What they did not do was attempt to challenge or falsify their hypotheses by testing triplets that they believed would not conform to their rule. Wason referred to this phenomenon as *confirmation bias*, whereby subjects systematically seek only evidence that confirms their hypotheses. Numerous other studies, both by Wason and colleagues,[55] and others,[56] have confirmed the persistence of this tendency.

The converse of confirmation bias is *motivated reasoning,* or the idea that we look more skeptically at data that don't fit with our beliefs than at those that do.[57] It is not difficult to imagine teacher evaluators being influenced positively by teachers who use strategies or methods of which the observer approves, while tending to be less generous with a teacher who teaches in ways that are not in their own repertoires.

Cognitive scientists have studied a second phenomenon that is relevant to the observation of classroom teaching behavior. *Inattentional blindness* is a striking occurrence in which people fail to notice stimuli appearing in front of their eyes when they are preoccupied with an attentionally demanding task.[58] In a particularly vivid experiment, over 200 undergraduates watched one of four videotapes, each 75 seconds in duration.[59] Each tape showed two teams of three players practicing basketball, one team wearing white shirts and the other wearing black shirts, who moved around in a relatively random fashion in an open area in front of a bank of three elevator doors. The members of each team passed or bounce-passed a basketball to one another in a regular order: Player 1 would pass to Player 2, who would pass to Player 3, who would pass to Player 1, and so on. Players would also dribble the ball, wave their arms, and make other movements consistent with their overall pattern of action, only incidentally looking directly at the camera. After about 45 seconds of this action, one of two unexpected events occurred: either a tall woman holding an open umbrella walked from off camera on one side of the action to the other, left to right, or a shorter woman wearing a gorilla costume that fully covered her body walked through the action in the same way. In both cases, the unexpected event lasted 5 seconds, and the players continued their actions during and after the event. Still shots from these videos are seen in Figure 4.1.

The students were asked to view the film clip and count the number of passes the members of one or other team made to each other. At least half the students failed to see the unexpected event under various experimental conditions. In one version, the gorilla stopped halfway across the display, turned to face the camera, thumped its chest, and then exited on the other side of the screen. Even in this condition, half of the observers did not see it. In fact, when the experimenters showed the video again after explaining what had occurred, observers were often shocked, sometimes even exclaiming, "I missed *that*?"[60]

An example of the same type is referenced by Gary Marcus in his recent book *Kluge.* Here, the English magician and illusionist Darren

Brown stops someone on the street and asks them directions using a map. While the two are pointing at the map and discussing directions, a man carrying a large flat object walks between them. At this moment an accomplice exchanges places with Darren Brown and, after the man has passed, continues the discussion with the helpful pedestrian, who fails to notice that she is no longer talking to the same man.[61]

We can take away the following message from these studies. If observers of a classroom are attending to a particular aspect of the lesson, such as the teacher's questioning strategies or the number of times students raise their hands, and they do not expect two students to be writing text messages back and forth to one another or to be engaged in some informal peer tutoring, then the observers are unlikely to notice those things.

The literature on information processing and perception points us to problems and challenges inherent in mental processes that are relevant to the act of observing human behavior in general and classroom teaching in particular. In a classic paper written in the 1950s called "The Magical Number Seven Plus or Minus Two," the psychologist George Miller was struck by a series of contemporary experiments that showed how our short-term memories restrict the amount of information we can handle in making absolute judgments.[62] He expressed this as *channel capacity*, or the upper limit on the extent to which an observer can match his or her responses to a given set of stimuli. Miller hypothesized that the findings from the different experiments he reviewed may be due to some common but unknown underlying mechanism. More than 50 years later we know a lot more about short-term memory. While Miller's paper underlines the importance of being aware of memory restrictions and channel capacity, we know there is a lot more to human memory performance than the characteristics of one subsystem. In fact, one could even say that the value 7 ± 2 as an absolute measure of short-term memory is an urban legend. It only applies to speakers of English attempting to remember a sequence of digits. Actual human memory performance depends on many factors and cannot be approximated by a numeric value.

Related to the idea of channel capacity is the concept of *bounded rationality* coined by the psychologist Herbert Simon around the same time that George Miller wrote his famous article.[63] Because of limits in human mental capacity, Simon posited, the mind cannot cope directly with the complexity of the world, so constructs a simplified mental model of reality from which to operate. In spite of behaving rationally within the bounds of our mental model, we are not always cognitively well equipped to deal with the requirements of the real world. The con-

Figure 4.1. Still frames from the Simons and Chabris Selective-looking Paradigm.

cept of bounded rationality has come to be recognized widely, though not universally, both as an accurate portrayal of human judgment and choice and as a reasonable explanation for how humans adjust to the limitations inherent in the mind's functioning.

An alternative approach views the perceptual process as hypothesis testing, where sometimes our hypotheses are wrong. We are often fooled by what we see because we incorporate our own cognitive distortions into our perceptions. The Scots psychologist R. L. Gregory maintains that there is a direct relation between the way we think abstractly and the way we perceive. He reviews a variety of illusions that illustrate how easily our perceptual judgment is fooled into forming conceptions of things that do not in fact exist. Two classic examples of these are the Necker cube (Figure 4.2), an ambiguous drawing of a cube that seems to reverse its orientation as we examine it, and the Müller-Lyer illusion (Figure 4.3), in which the shaft line with the outgoing arrow heads appears longer than that with the ingoing heads, even when we know both lines are the same length. As Gregory puts it, we tend to identify and act on objects in the environment not so much according to what is sensed, but what is believed.[64] Elsewhere, he poses the question, "How do we recognize the present, without confusion from the past?"[65]

Figure 4.2. The Necker Cube

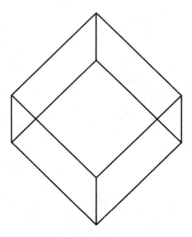

Figure 4.3. The Müller-Lyer Illusion

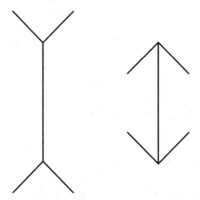

There are many examples throughout the psychological literature of the limitations in our human cognitive and perceptual capacities. Moreover, this research suggests that the ability to make accurate judgments is most difficult under exactly those circumstances that pertain when we are attempting to make evaluations of teaching behavior: that is, as we make judgments about evolving situations sometimes requiring multiple perspectives, on the basis of incomplete and ambiguous information that we must process incrementally, often under pressure for immediate judgment.

These circumstances in our mental processing abilities lead to what might be described as biases when we come to perform observations in the classroom or, indeed, anywhere else. Perception is not a passive and objective process where we record what is actually in front of us. In fact, our perceptions are influenced by our past experience, education, values, role, context, and prevailing organizational norms, so that we end up constructing our own reality rather than describing some objective phenomenon. Thus when you look at Figure 4.4, unless you have remarkable powers of observation or are familiar with the example, you probably do not notice the extra definite or indefinite articles. This illustrates the notion that we see what we expect to see. Once you do notice the extra word, hindsight bias makes it difficult to imagine that you ever missed it in the first place.

Another example showing the influence of context on perception is illustrated by Figures 4.5 and 4.6.[66] Most people will perceive the characters in Figure 4.5 as letters of the alphabet. However, the same characters in a different context will be perceived as a numeral.

Related to the same concept of seeing what you expect to see is the principle that it takes more information to recognize an unexpected than an expected phenomenon. Jerome Bruner and Leo Postman conducted a now classic experiment that demonstrates this.[67] They showed undergraduates images of playing cards, some of which were tricked out so that black suits were shown to be red and vice versa, thus introducing incongruous or unexpected data. They found that the students took longer to identify the unexpected or tricked-out versions than the standard versions, thus confirming their hypothesis:

> Perceptual organization is powerfully determined by expectations built upon past commerce with the environment. When such expectations are violated by the environment, the perceiver's behavior can be described as resistance to the recognition of the unexpected or incongruous.[68]

A principal, teacher educator, or educational researcher trying to make sense of the course of events as they observe a classroom is analogous to the test subject identifying playing cards. What is actually perceived, as well as how it is interpreted, depends in part at least on the observer's patterns of expectation. Educators do not just have expectations about the color of hearts and spades; they have a set of assumptions and expectations about teachers' and students' motivations and educational processes. Events consistent with these expectations are perceived and processed easily, while events that contradict them

Figure 4.4. We See What We Expect to See

tend to be ignored or distorted in perception. Of course this distortion is not a conscious process, as illustrated by how some readers will have ignored the extra word in Figure 4.4.

Another characteristic of perceptions or mind sets is that they are quick to form but resistant to change. Gerald Fischer demonstrated this in his work with ambiguous stimuli, such as the set of line drawings that could be perceived as a man's face (labeled with a lack of political correctness characteristic of the times as a "gypsy") or a girl with a mirror as in Figure 4.7. When test subjects are shown these figures their tendency to identify a drawing as a man or a girl is influenced by which end of the series they started from, or whether previously seen images had been identified as the male or female figure. This demonstrates that we assimilate new images onto existing images, with the tendency being stronger the more ambiguous the information is and the more confident we are of the validity of our image.

The Necker cube and similar ambiguous images demonstrate the difficulty of viewing the same information from different perspectives. In Figure 4.8, Fischer found that both interpretations of each ambiguous figure had an equal chance of being generated by observers. However, once you arrive at the first interpretation of the image it is difficult to switch to the other perspective. Yet, as an observer of classroom teaching, you may be required to view things from a student's perspective, the teacher's perspective, or principal's or researcher's point of view.

Sometimes the information is unclear because of substandard conditions, rather than because it is ambiguous. Jerome Bruner and Mary Potter explored this in a series of experiments during the early 1960s.[69] They showed subjects blurry images of familiar objects such as a fire hydrant or a dog on a lawn. The more time subjects had to formulate hypotheses from the blurry images, the slower they were to identify them correctly when the images were shown in better focus. Subjects who spent less time on the blurry images recognized them faster. This demonstrates that in contexts like these, the more information you

Figure 4.5. Perception and Context: 1

Figure 4.6. Perception and Context: 2

give someone, the more likely they are to generate inaccurate hypotheses, and the worse off they will be. Subsequently, it takes more information to reject the initial erroneous hypothesis than it did to generate it in the first place. We form impressions on the basis of very little information and then stick to them until we have overwhelming evidence that they are false. This is known as *belief perseverance*,[70] and has been found in several subsequent experiments, many of them from the fields of business and economics.[71]

One more relevant phenomenon, that of rationalization after the fact, is familiar to most of us. It is sometimes referred to as *hindsight bias*.[72] This describes the tendency to see events that have occurred as more predictable than they had been before they took place. Hindsight bias has been demonstrated experimentally in a variety of settings, including politics, law, and medicine. In psychological experiments of hindsight bias, subjects also tend to remember their predictions of future events as having been stronger than they actually were, in those cases where those predictions turn out to be correct.[73] In classroom settings hindsight bias may come into play when a principal reviews

Figure 4.7. The Man and The Girl

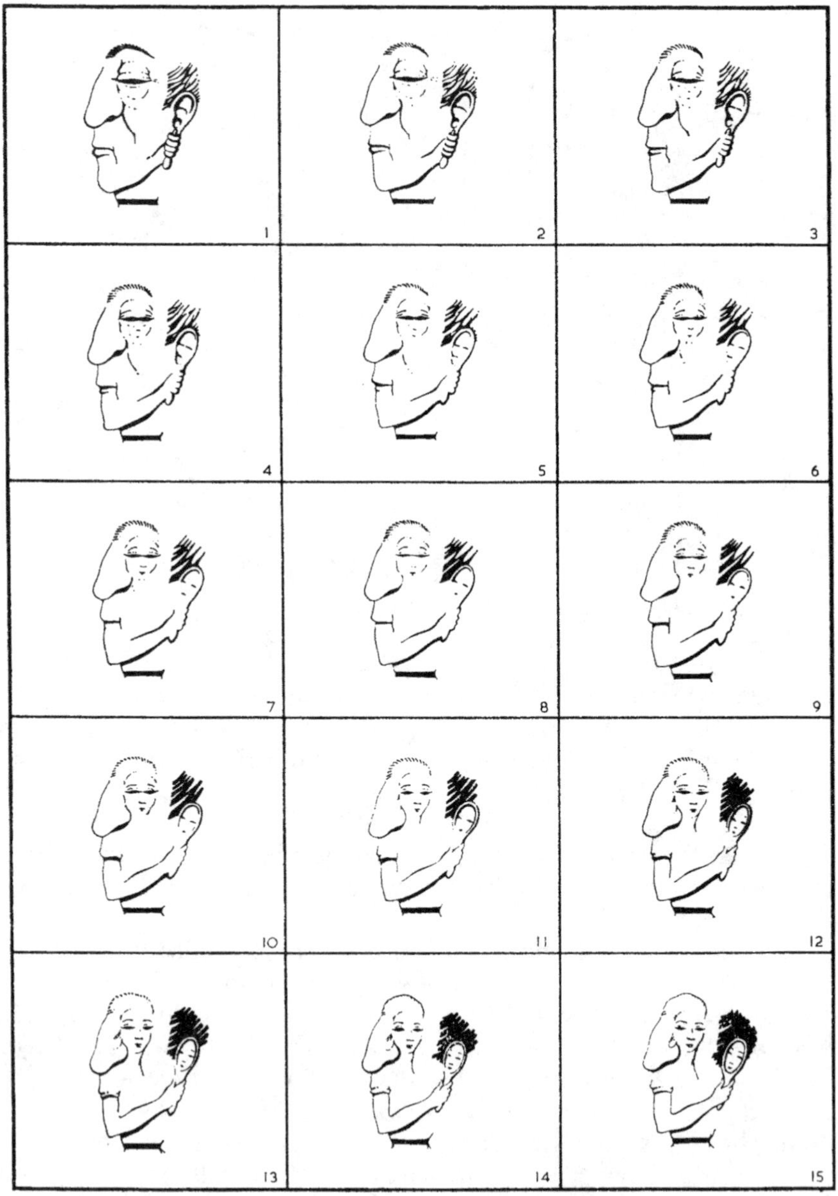

Source: Fischer, 1967.

Figure 4.8. Six Ambiguous Figures

Snail/elephant; Pirate/rabbit; Wife/mother-in-law;
Husband/Father-in-law; Duck/rabbit; Lion/rose

Source: Fischer, 1967.

an observational evaluation of a teacher after later receiving some new information about the teacher from a parent, student test scores, or by speaking with another observer of that teacher.

This brief look at some of the evidence from psychology and cognitive science raises more than a few alerts for anyone intending to conduct classroom observations for the purpose of evaluating or making judgments about teaching practice. Here is a summary of what this research tells educators:

- We tend to see what we expect to see.
- We tend to form judgments quickly, and they are highly resistant to change.
- We tend to make new information fit our existing conceptual framework.

- If we are focusing attention on one thing, we may not notice other things.
- Initial impressions formed from incomplete or ambiguous information are likely to persist even after better information becomes available.
- It is difficult to view the same information from different perspectives.
- We tend to misremember how we saw events originally in order to fit the way things eventually transpire.

With these phenomena in mind, let me finally consider some of the thinking about the cognitive mechanisms that influence how we make judgments, and hence how we evaluate teachers when we observe their teaching. Philosophers, dating back to Socrates, and psychologists over the past century[74] have discussed two generic modes of cognitive function that describe what we might think of as intuitive versus deliberate or rational thought processes. More recently researchers have further emphasized and defined the distinction between these "dual systems" of cognitive processes: those executed quickly with little conscious deliberation and those that are slower and more reflective.[75] Keith Stanovich and Richard West called these "System 1" and "System 2" processes, respectively.[76]

The operations of System 1 are fast, automatic, effortless, associative, and difficult to control or modify. It produces shortcuts, known as heuristics, that allow us to function rapidly and effectively. The popular book *Blink: The Power of Thinking Without Thinking* by the journalist Malcolm Gladwell, reviews a number of studies from various fields where so-called experts make System 1 judgments with great effectiveness.[77] However, Gladwell underestimates the potential for quick and dirty judgments to get us into trouble. A program of research studies conducted by Kahneman and colleagues (known now as the "heuristics and biases approach") has documented the persistence of systematic errors in the intuitions of experts, implying that their intuitive judgments may be endorsed, at least passively, by their rational processes from System 2, one of whose functions is to monitor the quality both of mental operations and overt behavior. These studies suggest that the monitoring is normally quite lax, and allows many erroneous intuitive judgments to be expressed, along with the correct ones. One study by Shane Frederick demonstrated this clearly.[78] He found that quite large percentages of highly intelligent college students failed to reject plausible but erroneous solutions to simple puzzles such as the following:

1. A bat and a ball cost $1.10 in total. The bat costs $1.00 more than the ball. How much does the ball cost? _____ cents
2. If it takes 5 machines 5 minutes to make 5 widgets, how long would it take 100 machines to make 100 widgets?_____ minutes
3. In a lake, there is a patch of lily pads. Every day, the patch doubles in size. If it takes 48 days for the patch to cover the entire lake, how long would it take for the patch to cover half of the lake? _____ days[79]

Respondents seem to have offered responses that were readily accessible without checking them. The surprisingly high rate of errors in these easy problems illustrates how lightly the output of System 1 is monitored by System 2.

The operations of System 2 are slower, serial, effortful, and deliberately controlled; they are also relatively flexible and potentially rule-governed. System 2 judgments are less often erroneous than System 1 judgments, and since the path to the result is conscious, errors can be corrected. Much of the unreliability in human judgment comes from our inability or disinclination to use it. This work is nicely described and summarized in Daniel Kahneman's Nobel Prize lecture from 2002.[80]

Thus in a classroom setting we can imagine that an observer will generate both System 1 and System 2 judgments. Even with an evaluation instrument that inclines an observer toward the conscious, rational judgments of System 2, unconscious System 1 judgments will be made as part of a cognitive process that needs to be considered in any analysis of observation protocols.

STUDIES OF THE EFFECTS OF MENTORING AND INDUCTION ON TEACHING PRACTICE

With this background we are now probably prepared to view data derived from classroom observations with a little more caution, if not skepticism, than previously. In fact, we might even be surprised if there are any viable studies at all that convincingly test the connection between mentoring or induction and teaching practice.

The title of a very recent review article, "Effects of Teacher Induction on Beginning Teachers' Teaching," led me to believe that I would find reference to all the latest studies that look at the connection between teacher induction support and teaching practice.[81] Jian Wang and his coauthors conducted an ERIC[82] search back to 1960, followed references generated by a previous search conducted for another article, and reviewed their personal collection for relevant papers, articles, and books. They divided the resulting body of work into three groups, reflecting different ways of hypothesizing how mentoring might affect beginning teachers' practice. The first group consists of writings that analyze what mentors do, or say they do, and that identify impacts on novices' practices based on "theoretical assumptions" of effective mentoring.[83] In other words, induction activities are explored through case studies, discourse analyses, surveys, and interviews, and then speculative connections are made to teaching behaviors. The second group of studies all derived their information from teachers' self-reports about how induction support influenced their teaching, gathered via surveys, journals, or structured interviews. Unfortunately, these self-reports amounted to no more than teachers' stated beliefs that things they valued such as observation of experienced teachers, discussions with mentors about their teaching, and reflections following mentor observations, were helpful in their work. We have no idea from these studies what aspects of teaching behavior were influenced, or what teachers actually did in the classroom. The final group of studies, according to the authors, "directly captured the relationship between particular program components and novice teachers' beliefs and teaching practice."[84] This means that the last category of studies looked at specific components of induction, such as workshops or subject-specific pedagogical support, and the researchers either speculated about teaching effects, or asked teachers via surveys or interviews about self-reported effects. In short, hardly any of the reviewed studies incorporated assessments based on observations of actual teaching behavior.

One exception was a study where 46 experienced teachers were randomly assigned either to receive or not to receive mentor training.[85] At the beginning of school, mentors were each assigned to work with a beginning teacher for the first half of the school year. The researchers videotaped mentor–novice conversations, collected weekly summaries of mentoring activities and their monthly goals, and conducted three to six lesson observations of beginning teachers' teaching. The study found that new teachers working with trained mentors had higher ratings on adjusting classroom activities to meet students' interests, establishing routines and procedures, and keeping students on task.

Wang and colleagues are quick to point out other shortcomings in the studies they reviewed, such as failing to account for school context factors, and assuming that the induction interventions were unilateral forces of influence over teachers' conceptions and hypothesized teaching practice. The authors conclude:

Research in this area is emerging but is insufficient in determining what preservice preparation is useful for learning to teach in various induction contexts. Comparative studies of induction experiences among beginning teachers who are from different types of preservice and alternative licensure programs are needed. To conduct these comparisons, research should be designed to survey and interview beginning teachers and observe their teaching practice.[86]

My own review of the literature uncovers only two recent studies connecting induction and/or mentoring to teaching practice that used observations of actual classroom teaching (among other measures) and that were not included in the review just discussed. The first study followed just six primary teachers over one year, collecting interview and observation data.[87] The authors used an observation protocol called AIMS that they had developed themselves. AIMS subscales included Classroom Atmosphere, Instruction/Content, and Management. Three of the teachers had school-based mentors only, while the other three also received support from a second mentor supplied by the researchers. They conducted observations three times at the beginning, middle, and end of the year. Cumulative changes in AIMS scores showed that "both groups of teachers declined in their use of effective teaching practices over the course of the year, with slightly greater average declines in the practices of teachers who received mentoring from only school-provided mentors."[88] This finding is hardly an endorsement for the effects of mentoring on teacher practice, and may quite likely exemplify the problems associated with classroom observation noted earlier.

The second study, conducted by researchers at Educational Testing Service (ETS), is worth describing in some detail, even though it has not appeared in a peer-reviewed journal, since it is unique in both approach and sample size, and makes a contribution for those reasons.[89] In 2002 ETS was commissioned by the California Commission on Teacher Credentialing (CCTC) to conduct a study of the impact of California's BTSA/CFASST, program (see Chapter 2). ETS designed a study that looked at the impact of the program on the teaching practices of beginning teachers and on the learning of their students. (I review the second part of that study in the next chapter.) The design of the study was quasi-experimental.[90] Since all new teachers in California receive BTSA support, they could not compare BTSA and non-BTSA teachers. Their strategy, because BTSA programs vary widely across the state, was to determine via questionnaires how much support teachers actually received, and group the respondents according to their level of "engagement" with the program. Their sample was third- to fifth-grade teachers in the third year of their careers. They surveyed some 1,125 teachers in order to find out about their experiences with BTSA and the formative assessment system CFASST (see Chapter 2 for a description of this). They received replies from only 287 teachers in 78 different BTSA programs (a paltry 26% response rate). They calculated a "CFASST engagement score" by classifying each teacher into high, middle, or low CFASST engagement levels. They then contacted a sub-sample of 64 respondents for further study, attempting to draw from the top and bottom of the CFASST engagement scale. These teachers were interviewed by phone for further information and to validate the survey results. From this group, they recruited a sub-sub-sample of 34 teachers for blind case studies involving two classroom observations per teacher and face-to-face interviews.

Using the observations and interviews, the ETS researchers developed ratings of teaching practice based on items from the California Standards for the Teaching Profession (CSTP) that would be observable in the classroom, together with other measures of teaching practice.[91] By linking these measures of teaching practice with the CFASST engagement ratings derived from the survey, they tested for a relationship between BTSA/CFASST engagement and teaching practice. Their research hypothesis was that the higher a teacher's CFASST engagement level, the stronger their teaching practices would be.

They rated the following elements of teaching practice from the observation and interview data:

- Instructional planning (Interview)
- Reflection on practice (Interview)
- Questioning practices (Observation): Proportion of questions asked that are
  —At the deep level
  —At the intermediate level
  —Open-ended
- Feedback practices (Observation): Proportion of feedback instances that are
  —Positive
  —Instructional in focus
  —Substantive and specific
- Depth of student understanding (Interview)
- Scores on the CSTP from Description of Practice (DOP)(Observation)

Interviews were coded for the target information and scored. Three researchers conducted all the observations and a fourth reviewed all the tapes. Interrater agreement was calculated before observers and raters conducted calibrating conversations, and agreement was recalculated, yielding fairly high but somewhat inconsistent levels of reliability. The authors discussed various weaknesses in their observation and interview data and processes. These ranged from lack of clarity about the definition of items, to fatigue problems handling the coding of observations on the same day they were collected, bias in the selection of students for interview as well as the unreliability of the insights of younger students, and the sheer number of items from the CSTP/DOP instrument along with its high degree of inference. Add to these issues the fact that observations were based on one lesson only (and for the questioning items, just 20 minutes of a lesson) and that the overall study design did not allow for random assignment to groups, and we are left doubting both the reliability and validity of the results. The authors duly acknowledge these challenges, but are not discouraged from reporting their findings.

In their analyses of the data they found that the high and low CFASST engagement groups differed statistically in one variable only: Instructional planning. They also reported that the high CFASST engagement teachers outscored the low group on six of the other nine measures of teaching practice, but the differences were not statistically significant. The authors conclude that, overall, their results demonstrate "a positive impact of BTSA/CFASST on teachers."[92]

This seems a rather generous conclusion, if only because the high- and low-engagement groups were generated using survey data from teachers about their involvement with induction programs, based on a 26% response rate. How typical were these 26% who took the trouble to respond? Without random assignment, these groups could reflect factors other than BTSA involvement. For example, schools with well-developed, comprehensive induction programs might have other resources such as teacher aides, strong grade-level or subject-matter collaboration, an involved parent community, and positive working conditions in general. Any of these other factors may influence a teacher's classroom behavior as much or more than the BTSA program.

Nevertheless, it should be recognized that this is the only study to be found that attempts to use multiple sources of data, including classroom observation, to measure teacher practice, while sampling teachers from a wide variety of school districts and programs. Also, the authors were quite conscious of the study's limitations and discuss them in their reports.

So that's all we have to go on—one study with severe limitations that uses observational data, and other studies that invite speculation on the theoretical effects on practice based on evidence about what mentors do when they work with beginning teachers or what they believe is important about teaching, or self-reports from teachers about how induction in general or specific components of induction programs influence their thinking about teaching or their classroom practice.

ASSESSING THE EVIDENCE: DOES TEACHER INDUCTION AFFECT THE DEVELOPMENT OF TEACHING PRACTICE?

The evidence is convincing, if not surprising, that teachers are important for student learning. In considering the definition of teacher quality and teacher effectiveness, we must distinguish, as Fenstermacher and Richardson have pointed out, good from successful teaching. Unfortunately, in spite of a widespread movement to identify teaching standards, we are still not that close to being able to determine exactly what makes a good teacher (as distinct from good teaching), given the complexity of the work and the wide variety of conditions under which it is performed. In our search for high-quality teachers, we would do well to ignore factors related to their education and experience and pay attention to what they do in the classroom and their record for improving student learning through increasing standardized test scores. It is helpful to think of these concepts as related either to "inputs" (teacher qualifications and characteristics), "process" (teacher practices), and "outcomes" (teacher effectiveness). Focusing on outcomes, William Sanders' research emphasizes the long-lasting effects on students of having an effective or ineffective teacher for 3 years in a row. However, this leaves us in the somewhat circular position of defining effective teachers as those who are effective. In most circumstances we are not in a position to wait several years to review the value-added data on student achievement, even if they are available, in order to evaluate teacher effectiveness. What we need to be able to do is to link teacher practices with teacher effectiveness so that we can predict effectiveness by looking at practice. Thus we are exhorted by Dan Goldhaber and Emily Anthony to rely on classroom observations to assess the teacher practices (and characteristics) that may be associated with student learning.

Evidence from the fields of psychology and cognitive science, however, leads us to be wary about the reliability of any judgments of teaching behavior that we might make during classroom observations. Observation instruments developed for educational purposes do not make allowances for cognitive and perceptual restrictions, and most are not specifically developed to measure features that are the explicit focus of induction programs. Add to this the difficulty in deciding how much and what kind of teaching behavior needs to be sampled and we understand the challenges of evaluating teacher quality in this manner. The alternative method of polling teachers' self-reports about their teaching practice through interviews or surveys is likely to be unreliable and to reflect bias. The few studies that may provide insights into any connection between induction support and beginning teacher practice rely almost wholly on self-report data. A thorough review of the literature reveals only one or two research studies that have attempted to investigate this relationship through classroom observational methods.

Recent trends toward standards-based teaching have produced assessment systems such as the Danielson *Framework* that include observation of teaching along with other sources of information. Some studies have shown a weak relation between the *Framework* and student learning in some settings, but yield no insights into the possible connection between induction support and development of teaching practice. Thus we must conclude that the jury is out on the degree to which induction programs may have a direct effect on teaching performance. The limited evidence that is available mostly from self-report data allow us to hypothesize that induction support, or certain components of induction programs, may reasonably be affecting teachers' attitudes to their work, or their actual classroom practice, but definitive empirical substantiation is lacking. Common sense and anecdotal reports lead us to expect that mentoring and induction for beginning teachers would influence the way they work in the classroom, but the difficulties of setting up an experimental study, the problems of observational research, and the unreliability of teacher self-reports force us to conclude that we really do not know the extent or nature of any effects of induction on teaching, and what we think we know, we cannot prove.

Chapter 5

Induction Programs and Their Effect on Student Achievement

THE MEASUREMENT OF STUDENT ACHIEVEMENT

Perhaps the single most frequently asked question from school administrators and legislators who are considering budgeting funds for an induction program is whether implementation of the program is likely to result in positive student academic outcomes. In an era when test scores are everything, and schools and teachers are increasingly evaluated according to their school's Adequate Yearly Progress (AYP),[1] instituted by the No Child Left Behind Act, the impetus behind many school reforms is directed toward raising student achievement scores as evidence that student learning is increasing. Some fear that this sometimes encourages a teach-to-the-test mentality that can result in test scores that are not an accurate measurment real student learning.

Since the activities of an induction program are at least one step removed from the students, it is challenging to design research that can test the existence of a causal relationship between new teacher induction and student achievement. The concept of student achievement itself is also not without controversy. Usually portrayed by scores on standardized tests, student achievement represents evidence of student academic learning, the primary goal of schooling. Other outcomes that have been used as evidence of student learning include grades, graduation rates,[2] percentage of students taking advanced placement classes,[3] and analysis of student work products.[4]

Over the last 10 years or so, the most popular outcome measure of student learning (under protest from some educators) has been adjusted gains in standardized test scores, computed as a value-added measure of teacher effectiveness. The advantage of this method is that it looks at student progress rather than the level of achievement. No matter which of the several statistical options for value-added modeling (VAM) a researcher uses, however, there are some cautions to consider. First, since neither students nor teachers are randomly assigned to classes and schools, any thorough model should find some way to take into account the school, class, and other factors that might influence student performance. For example, parents may select school districts, schools, and even teachers; teachers may choose which students are assigned to their classes; district resources may be differentially distributed among schools; classroom climates and other contextual conditions may vary. In addition, data may be missing from district databases. Some VAMs attempt to make statistical corrections for these factors, but it is impossible to identify and model all of them, and their influence on student outcomes may be as powerful as anything the teacher does in the classroom.

Any failure to reconcile the influence of non-school-related factors in what amounts to quasi experiments of teacher or school performance confounds the causal inferences educators are looking to make and produces estimates of teacher or school performance together with that of the exogenous variables. Controlling for exogenous variables may be achieved through research design or statistical controls, or both. While the statistical methods can be applied to the analysis of quasi-experimental data (i.e., nonrandom data sets), they can never fully isolate the impact of the school from other factors believed to affect a student's test score. Another issue that has been discussed (by Dale Ballou[5] among others) concerns the fact that test questions are not all of equal difficulty, so that a 10-point gain for a student at the lower end of the continuum is not necessarily comparable to a 10-point gain for a higher performing student. This has led some to conclude that we should not attempt to compare gains at different places on the scale for a given population.[6]

A recent paper by Jesse Rothstein[7] (not published at the time of writing, but available online) challenges VAMs by conducting a falsification analysis whereby he uses VAM data to test whether a future teacher has as much effect on student gains as the current teacher. His study showed that fifth-grade teachers had nearly as much effect on fourth-grade gains as on fifth-grade gains. Put somewhat simplistically, his analysis argues for the importance of the random assignment of teachers to classes in order to establish any causal relation between teacher and value-added scores.

I will not go into the exotic workings performed by statisticians who refine value-added analyses in an attempt to address some of the issues that critics have raised. However, it is important to get a flavor of the differences among principal approaches to value-added modeling. For those readers with a good knowledge of statistics, I recommend an article and a monograph by Daniel McCaffrey from the Rand Corporation (both written with colleagues), that discuss many of the finer points about the different methods for estimating value-added effectiveness.[8] For the lay reader, I give here a simplified description of two versions that are in use in different states.

The most well-known VAM work has been done by Sanders[9] and his colleagues, who developed the Tennessee Value-Added Assessment System (TVAAS).[10] The TVAAS, or Education Value-Added Assessment System (EVAAS) as it is now known (since it is used in other states also), uses what Sanders calls the *layered model*,[11] because the data for later years are added or "layered" on to the model for earlier years. The basic model consists of an equation that expresses the score of a student at the end of a particular grade in a particular year as the sum of the district average for that grade and year, a class or teacher effect, and systematic and unsystematic variations. In this manner, the basic difference between the student's score and the average district score is attributed to a "class effect" plus the combined contributions of unspecified variations, including measurement errors. It is assumed that the class effect is the same for all the students in the class and attributable to the teacher of that class, thus to be labeled the "teacher effect." When the student moves to the next year and the next grade, the model then consists of four components: the district average for that grade and year, the teacher effect for that year, the teacher effect for the previous year, and the systematic and unsystematic variations. In order to conduct these analyses it is necessary to be able to keep track of students linked to teachers over different grades, subjects, and years.

Several criticisms have been leveled at TVAAS/EVAAS in the 10 years that it has existed. Perhaps most often mentioned is that TVAAS excludes student background characteristics such as gender, race, and poverty level.[12] Sanders maintains it is not necessary to control for student characteristics because each student is considered to be his or her own control.[13] As a result, he claims, the correlations between student characteristics and gains (as opposed to simple achievement) are close to zero, because the influence of factors such as socioeconomic status on the posttest scores are already reflected in the pretest scores. Dale Ballou wanted to test this assertion and collaborated with Sanders on a study of data from one school district. Their analysis confirmed that race, gender, and poverty had only a minor effect on teacher effectiveness as measured by VAM.[14] This minor effect, nevertheless, had an influence on whether a teacher succeeded or failed to reach a preset performance standard. Without the socioeconomic and demographic controls, more than one third of the teachers dropped out of the top 10% stratum that had been created with the controls in place. Unfortunately, this one study of a single school district is not sufficient to support the assumption that student characteristics can be ignored, or to confirm that it needs to be included. One other study suggests that Sanders may be overstating the irrelevance of student characteristics when looking at gains. Tom Kane and Douglas Staiger analyzed North Carolina value-added data and found that students with more educated parents not only had higher baseline scores but also made greater improvement from year to year.[15]

One of the most thorough critics of the TVAAS is Haggai Kupermintz, who, in addition to making the above point and asserting that, in fact, much of Sanders's own data appear to contradict this claim, sees several other weaknesses in the approach.[16] One problem for Kupermintz, which amounts to a criticism of VAM in general, not just the TVAAS/EVAAS, is the circularity inherent in the identification of student gains as both the definition and the measurement of teacher effectiveness:

> In other words, differences in student learning *determines*—by definition—teacher effectiveness: a teacher whose students achieve larger gains is the "effective teacher." TVAAS divides teachers into five "effectiveness" groups according to their ranking among their peers in terms of average student gains. To turn full circle and claim that teacher effectiveness is the *cause* of student score gains is at best a necessary, trivial truth similar to the observation that "all bachelors are unmarried."[17]

Kupermintz also disapproves of the way TVAAS deals with missing data (it estimates teachers with missing data as close to the district mean), the fact that it ignores the possibility of multiple teachers influencing student test scores during a given year (for example, a science teacher and a math teacher both influencing math performance), and the fact that it inadequately addresses within-class differences in student ability to produce robust gains. In summary, Kupermintz questions the validity of using mixed models that are designed for agricultural or experimental data to address education questions.

Another common complaint that has been leveled at Sanders is the lack of transparency of his methods. Critics protest that there has been no independent review of its underlying methodology because Sanders guards it as proprietary and holds it in secret. Kupermintz recommends that the TVAAS database be made available, along with all technical documentation, to interested researchers and that national standards and mechanisms be developed for the approval of statistical procedures and models that are used in high-stakes accountability systems.

The most recent article to appear expressing concerns about EVAAS is by Audrey Amrein-Beardsley of Arizona State University and published in the *Educational Researcher*, the flagship journal of the American Educational Research Association (AERA).[18] She, too, objects to the shortage of external peer reviews and validity studies of the model, bemoans its "insufficient user-friendliness," and highlights methodological issues about missing data, regression to the mean, and student background variables. Taking a step beyond that of previous critics, Amrein-Beardsley goes on to reanalyze data from an unpublished report by Sanders and colleagues[19] comparing National Board Certified Teachers (NBCTs) with non-NBCTs. Where Sanders found no difference in the student achievement of NBCT and non-NCBT classes, Amrein-Beardsley's reanalysis found a significant difference. She pointed out that Sanders focused on the smaller number of negative differences in the data while ignoring the larger number of positive differences. She concluded that "Sanders's more sophisticated value-added analyses just (a) reduced the numbers of statistically significant findings and (b) weakened effect sizes."[20]

A second version of VAM is the Dallas Value-Added Accountability System (DVAAS) which has been employed by the Dallas school system for several years.[21] It conducts value-added analyses in order to identify not only highly effective teachers but also those who may need support. The DVAAS differs from the Sanders model in four important respects. First, it includes an adjustment for student-level characteristics. Second, it does not combine data across several grades, modeling only the relationship between adjusted test scores in adjacent grades. Third, it does not model gains in the adjusted test scores directly, opting instead for the estimate of a more general structural connection between them. Fourth, it includes a number of factors in addition to the teacher's contribution to student achievement to account for the influence of the school on test score changes.

Whichever way one decides to estimate teacher effects through value-added modeling, there are constraints attached to any implications that may be drawn. Given potential shortcomings related to the statistical power of a particular model, omitted background variables, missing data, limitations of the achievement test itself, the circular logic of defining effectiveness as academic gain, and sampling error, we should be wary of using VAM for any high-stakes evaluation of teachers. It has been suggested that VAM be restricted to evaluations of schools and districts rather than teachers,[22] that it is not well suited to secondary level teachers,[23] and that it should not be used as the sole measure in the summative evaluation of teachers. This last point is acknowledged by Sanders himself, albeit with a different rationale:

> As to summative uses, a rigorous value-added approach is the fairest, most objective way to hold districts and schools accountable. At the teacher level, the value-added estimates of teacher effectiveness should be a part of formal teacher evaluation, but they should not be the sole basis upon which teachers are evaluated, because there are too many other duties, dimensions, and responsibilities that cannot be measured by a process such as [TVAAS/EVAAS].[24]

In spite of this caution, EVAAS is used in an increasing number of settings for teacher evaluation and teacher incentives. In Ohio, for example, under guidance from the nonprofit organization Battelle for Kids, the legislature adopted implementation of a value-added progress measure as an official metric in Ohio's education accountability system in 2007–08. As a result, all Ohio school districts receive fourth- to eighth-grade reading and math value-added reports. Florida has the School Accountability Report (SAR), which issues letter grades to all Florida schools based on measured levels of achievement and growth in reading, math, and writing from the Florida Comprehensive Assessment Test (FCAT). Taking advantage of this state database, the mayor of St. Petersburg instituted a High School Principal Incentive Program, which provides financial bonuses to principals and assistant principals whose schools improve their SAR ratings. Other states including Arkansas and Delaware are joining the value-added bandwagon. In a 2007 *Education Week* article David Hoff reported that the federal government, under NCLB, is planning to spend $400 million to enable states to create data warehouses that allow for value-added assessments that would help determine schools' AYP and evaluate teachers' effectiveness.[25]

STUDIES OF THE CONNECTION BETWEEN INDUCTION PROGRAMS AND STUDENT ACHIEVEMENT

It is not difficult to see that there are serious challenges for any researcher who sets out to test the relationship between new-teacher induction programs and student achievement. A comparison between groups of teachers with and without the induction program under study would ideally involve random assignment, a condition that is rarely possible in the real world. To use VAM for the measure of teacher effectiveness requires access to suitable test data from the school district linking teachers to students over multiple years. Even if the data are available, one is open to all the criticisms of VAM discussed earlier. Alternative measures of student achievement have their own disadvantages. It is not surprising, therefore, to find that few attempts have been made to explore this relationship.

Let us start by looking at the ETS study of the California BTSA program described in the previous chapter. The reader will recall that ETS researchers began their study by surveying 1,125 third-year teachers from 78 California BTSA programs in 107 districts to find out the degree of their engagement with the BTSA/CFASST programs (i.e., how intensive was the induction intervention). They received responses from 287 teachers (26%) and then collected student achievement test data for the students of teachers who responded to the survey in an attempt to test for any relation between BTSA engagement and evidence of student learning. Because school districts own their test data, the researchers had to negotiate with each one in order to retrieve the relevant scores. Those that agreed to collaborate did not use standardized formats, thus resulting in further loss of information. They ended up with usable data for the students of only 144 of the 287 survey respondents, reducing their sample to 13%. They then linked the student test scores (California used the CAT-6[26] that year as well as the California Standards Tests, CST)[27] with the group assignment that represented the degree of engagement with BTSA/CFASST (high, medium, or low) in order to test for a relationship. They hypothesized that the higher the induction engagement level, the higher would be the students' standardized test scores.

An alert reader will notice at once that the ETS researchers were not looking at student gain scores (those would have been even more difficult to obtain from multiple districts), so the issues related to VAM, either its advantages or disadvantages, do not enter the picture. Absent also from the methodology is any element of random assignment. To control for school-level effects, they used the school Academic Performance Index (API) scores as a covariate. They employed hierarchical linear modeling (HLM)[28] to examine the relative contributions of the student-level variables—disability status, socioeconomic status (SES), and English-language-learner (ELL) status—and engagement with BTSA/CFASST, nested within individual teachers' classrooms. They report that, across all six subtests of the CAT-6 and the CSTs, the students of teachers who had a high level of engagement with BTSA/

CFASST outscored the students of teachers with a low level of engagement with the program, after controlling for API. They conclude that, although none of the score differences was statistically significant, the consistency of the results across all tests suggest that "BTSA/CFASST has a positive impact on student test scores."[29]

Given the many limitations of the study (most of which the authors recognize themselves), this may be considered a somewhat optimistic claim. No random assignment, very low response rates, estimates of intensity of induction based on self-report, lack of availability of data, and a focus on class level of achievement rather than student progress, combine to make us question the conclusion that any findings can suggest a causal relation between induction support and student achievement. To cap it off, none of the differences between the high- and low-intensity induction groups was statistically significant. While the researchers are to be applauded for taking on a monumentally difficult task, we must reserve judgment as to whether their study reveals anything notable about the possible connection between induction and student achievement.

I have conducted a couple of studies with my colleagues at the New Teacher Center at the University of California, Santa Cruz.[30] As noted earlier, difficulty accessing student achievement data linked to teachers is one of the major challenges to conducting value-added research. We were fortunate to have access to data from three California school districts with different kinds of induction programs that we could then compare. Since there was no random selection or assignment involved, the design may be described as quasi-experimental.[31] The three districts differed in size and student demographics. The largest district was four times the size of the smallest. One district had a population of about 25% Latino compared with about 80% in the other two districts. Similar differences held with regard to poverty. These variables, then, needed to be controlled for in the statistical analysis. All three districts had the same reading curriculum. The induction programs varied among the three districts according to how they were implemented in the teachers' second year. All three districts used full-release mentors with caseloads of 1:15 in the first year. In the second year, one district shifted to an in-school "buddy" mentor with no release time, one doubled the mentor caseload in the second year, and the third maintained the 1:15 caseload, thereby preserving the same intensity of induction support.

Using HLM, we found that the third district showed higher class reading gains for its beginning teachers than the other two districts, and that the type of induction model explained more of the variance than class poverty or minority status. In an alternative way of explaining the data, we showed that a student of a teacher in the high-intensity program would be predicted to gain between six and eight points in reading, but a student of teachers in the low intensity programs would lose points.

The second study, reported in the same article, compared beginning teachers in the high-intensity program with experienced teachers in the same schools. For this analysis, 5 years of achievement data were available. For each year, we calculated a gain score for every student using the normal curve equivalent (NCE) scores[32] from two successive testing periods. We also calculated the district preclass average for all students and all years. We then aggregated student scores to the class level. The data were then plotted using each class' prescore, the class gain, and the teacher's years of experience. To simplify the figure, we combined teachers based on how long they had been teaching, with novices working 2 years or less, mid-careers working 3–9 years, and veterans working 10 years or more. We excluded teachers' class scores for the time their years of experience transitioned them to another category (i.e., when they went from 2 to 3 years and 9 to 10 years of experience). We found that, although novice teachers were assigned low-achieving classes, they had, on average, greater achievement than more experienced teachers. Once again, it must be stressed that there was no random assignment or random selection, and any apparent connections between induction and student achievement should be interpreted with caution.

In a recent push for randomized controlled trial (RCT) [33] studies, the Institute of Education Sciences at the U. S. Department of Education opened a competition in 2004 for an RCT study of high-intensity induction programs. The grant was awarded to Mathematica Policy Research (MPR) for a 5-year study they called "The Impact Evaluation of Teacher Induction."[34] The researchers set out to investigate five research questions: What types of induction services are delivered and at what cost? Does induction raise the teacher retention rate? What are the characteristics of those retained versus those who leave? Does induction affect teacher practices? Does induction affect student performance? These questions represent all the biggest challenges in this line of research.

On reading the report on the study's design, one is further impressed by their ambitious intentions to be thorough and comprehensive in every aspect of the work. They are conducting classroom observations as well as collecting artifacts of teaching to assist them in measuring teacher practice. They are looking at retention longitudinally, not just after one year, and are distinguishing between movers, within and between districts, and leavers, both permanent and temporary. They are estimating adjusted student achievement gains in order to create teacher value-added scores. They will then combine value-added and classroom observation information to produce a teacher quality indicator that they will then link back to the retention information to see if the high-intensity programs are not only retaining more teachers, but retaining more high-quality teachers. They are focusing on two intensive induction programs as treatments, the NTC model (discussed in Chapter 2) and the ETS Pathwise model[35] (that has since been transferred to Greenlight for Learning). As controls they are using the prevailing induction programs in the districts under study. In other words, they are comparing high-intensity induction with some kind of default induction, rather than no induction at all.

With regard to site selection, MPR targeted districts according to size and poverty in order to assure large enough numbers of beginning teachers and to focus on districts with potentially high turnover rates. After eliminating districts that already had implemented high-intensity induction, had no interest in doing so, or who refused to participate for other reasons, they ended up with a final sample of 17 school districts. Schools with eligible beginning teachers in tested elementary grades were randomly assigned to one or the other of the two treatment models in a process known as *cluster random assignment*.[36] This allowed them to avoid having two teachers in the same school in differing experimental groups. The original plan called for the intervention to be studied for a single year, but this was revised when they acknowledged that the NTC model requires 2 years of implementation. Surveys and the monitoring of an outside evaluator provided a check that the high-intensity programs were, in fact, being implemented faithfully. Student achievement gains will be computed and the value-added scores of treatment and control teachers compared. Such a design does not come cheap, and not too many researchers have funding upwards of $14 million to enable them to conduct such an extensive experimental study. Unfortunately, as of the spring of 2008, no findings have been reported from even the first year of intervention.[37]

Jonah Rockoff's study of New York City data that was referenced in Chapter 3 also examined effects of mentoring on student achievement.[38] He was not able to compare new teachers that were in the induction program with new teachers that were not in the program, since all new teachers were enrolled. However, he was able to look at data for both new and experienced teachers, and, within the mentored group, those who received more or less time with a mentor. Overall, he found no relationship between mentoring and student achievement, but he did discover that those teachers who received more hours of mentoring had higher student achievement scores in both math and reading than those who had fewer hours. This is interesting in that the mentors had higher caseloads than recommended by the NTC model, suggesting that they might not have been able to provide equal or sufficient support to all their beginning teachers. It is possible that those teachers who did receive the requisite amount of attention from their mentors had students who recorded higher achievement gains. As an economist by training, Rockoff used a fixed effects model[39] to analyze the test score data, making his analysis vulnerable to the criticisms leveled by Rothstein against VAM analysis where there is no random assignment.

To date, these are the only studies that have attempted to investigate whether mentoring and induction have an effect on student achievement. A search of the literature reflects a similar paucity of studies that have examined the relation between professional development, broadly defined, and student achievement. This is not unexpected, since the same challenges apply to the study of teacher professional development and student achievement as to the study of teacher induction and student achievement, namely access to data, control of intervening variables, and difficulty of arranging for random assignment. Of possible relevance is a study conducted some years ago by John Ross from the Ontario Institute for Studies in Education, because the kind of professional development in question was coaching.[40] Eighteen history teachers in a small Ontario school district had access to coaching during the introduction of a new history curriculum. Teachers varied in how much they took advantage of the coaching during the treatment period. After pre- and posttests of students' history knowledge there was found to be a correlation between amount of coaching and student achievement. Given the limitations of sample size and study design (no randomization, and use of coaching determined by self-report) no conclusions about causality can be drawn. Also, the coaching did not involve classroom observation and coaches were given just 2 days of in-service training.

ASSESSING THE EVIDENCE:
DOES TEACHER INDUCTION AFFECT STUDENT ACHIEVEMENT?

The most widely adopted method for estimating school and teacher effectiveness is VAM, but, at the same time, it may also be the most controversial. Its advantages are that it uses a metric that is now part of the federal requirements for public schools, namely student test scores, and it focuses on student progress (in the form of gains on standardized tests) as opposed to simple achievement (scores at a given point in time). Its disadvantages are that it requires better data management systems than many districts have in place, uses elaborate statistical methods to compute results, uses a variety of methodological options that may not be transparent and about whose relative effectiveness there is no consensus, and relies entirely on test scores that may not truly reflect the extent of student learning. While the disadvantages of VAM may outnumber the advantages, the technique is rapidly gaining in popularity, and, used conservatively, may contribute to our ability to compare the effectiveness of schools and teachers.

The difficulties of making judgments about effectiveness are accentuated when applied to the question of whether induction programs influence student learning. Even if the conditions are in place to make the necessary assessments about the value added by teachers or schools to student test scores, it is rarely possible to set up an experimental condition with random selection and assignment that allows for the comparison of groups of teachers in different program conditions. The one study that has received the necessary funding to do this has yet to publish its findings.

Other studies that made various kinds of compromises on the ideal, either with a quasi-experimental design or by using an alternative to VAM, indicate a possible connection between comprehensive induction programs and student achievement, but are by no means definitive. The good news is that we have a clear understanding of the approaches that are necessary in order for us to determine whether there is a relationship, but the frustration is that we still lack any studies that answer the question for us.

Chapter 6

The Costs and Benefits of Induction and Mentoring Programs

BENEFIT-COST ANALYSIS

There had been no benefit-cost studies of induction programs for beginning teachers until my colleague and I at the New Teacher Center published one in 2007.[1] The purpose of this research was to provide legislators, educational administrators, and program leaders with the kind of economic information they might be able to use to make informed decisions about whether it might be worthwhile to fund induction programs for new teachers.

Benefit-cost analysis is an analytic tool used by economists to measure the life-cycle costs and benefits of competing alternative approaches, expressing value in monetary terms. One textbook on the subject notes:

> Benefit cost analysis is a framework for organizing thoughts, or considerations: nothing more, nothing less. For any real world choice, there will always be some considerations that cannot be easily enumerated or evaluated, where the analysis becomes quite conjectural. Benefit cost analysis does not, and should not, try to hide this uncertainty.[2]

Benefit-cost analyses, simply stated, estimate the financial benefits of a given course of action against the actual costs, and use the resulting balance to guide or evaluate decision making. Costs are either one-time or ongoing. Benefits are most often received over time. In its simple form, benefit-cost analysis is carried out using only actual financial costs and financial benefits. A more sophisticated approach attempts also to put a financial value on intangible costs and benefits, a process that can be highly subjective.

Benefit-cost analysis is traditionally linked to the familiar economic criteria of the *Pareto efficiency*,[3] which refers to a choice that makes at least one person better off without making anyone worse off. This is a difficult standard to maintain, since almost all public programs will make someone worse off, and it raises the possibility that a program under evaluation may not be undertaken when it in fact has merit. This is an example of a Type 1 error. Type 1 errors occur when programs succeed in delivering a valued service but the terms for measuring their impact are too stringent, leading to its rejection as policy decision.

Alternatively, under a somewhat looser standard called the *Kaldor-Hicks criterion*,[4] one need show only that the best choice is a potential Pareto improvement, that is to say that the winners could, in principle, compensate the losers, even though the losers need never actually be compensated (i.e., wealth maximization rather than utility maximization).[5] Under the Kaldor-Hicks interpretation, the likelihood of making a Type 1 error decreases while the possibility of a Type 2 error is introduced. Type 2 errors occur when programs fail to deliver, but the terms for measuring impact are too relaxed causing a program to be considered beneficial when in fact it should have been rejected.

One may immediately perceive that benefit-cost analysis is, at best, an imperfect science. Some have gone further to posit that it is even an immoral way of informing regulatory decision making.[6] Harvard professor Steven Kelman argued, with respect to health, safety, and environment regulatory decisions, that undertaking an act if its benefits outweigh its costs follows the doctrine of utilitarian moral philosophers, thus leading at times to untenable recommendations to perform acts whose benefits outweigh their costs, but are morally wrong, or to reject acts that are morally right because their costs outweigh their benefits. In a reply to Kelman, Robert Solow of MIT pointed out that benefit-cost analysis is not applied without constraint. Indeed, it is needed only when society is giving up some of one good thing in order to get more of another good thing, and that treatises on the theory and practice of cost-benefit analysis make it clear that certain ethical or political principles may trump any monetary advantages that are captured by mathematical estimates of gain or loss.[7]

Kelman also discusses the technical problems of assigning monetary values to benefits that have no traded market value, and maintains that the act of placing a price on things may essentially decrease their value. This criticism of benefit-cost analysis has been labeled the *saliency mismatch.*[8] Since some costs and some benefits are too difficult to calculate, it is possible that what is quantifiable may drown out what is not. In the absence of any alternative evaluative criterion, however, this might be the best we can do.

I do not intend here to contribute to any debate regarding the morality of adopting benefit-cost practices. Rather, I take the perspective that one may employ the economic practice of benefit-cost analysis to enable educational decision makers to evaluate the merits of an intervention (in this case an induction program for beginning teachers) with regard to its potential return on investment, under the assumption that no moral or ethical principle is violated. Most people, if asked whether teachers should receive teaching support or mentoring during their first two years in the classroom, would probably vote in favor.

Although nobody else has conducted a benefit-cost analysis of mentoring programs for beginning teachers, there have been several studies since the mid 1990s on benefit-cost relationships in other areas of education. For example, an Australian study evaluated the social benefits and costs of a flow of Fijian postgraduates studying in Australia;[9] a state study examined the costs and benefits of nutrition education programs in the state of Virginia;[10] other researchers examined Web-based training and estimated the number of students needed to recover costs over a 5-year period;[11] yet another study involved an estimation of the relative costs and benefits of year-round versus traditional educational programs;[12] and a number of studies have been conducted over the years to examine the investment value of preschool programs and early childhood care, some of which are described in more detail below. These include the Abecedarian program;[13] the Chicago Child-Parent Centers;[14] and the Perry Preschool Program.[15] There is also a literature covering the return on investment of training programs in general.[16] The existence of studies such as these serves to legitimize this kind of analysis for educational interventions.

Barbara Hummel-Rossi and Jane Ashdown surveyed the state of cost-benefit analysis in education as of 2002.[17] Their article is important for several reasons. First, they make a case for applying economic analyses to evaluate educational interventions. Second, they lay out clearly the methodological issues that are critical to cost-effectiveness studies in education, emphasizing the complexities inherent in assessing the inputs and outputs of education compared with other public policy fields such as hospital admission procedures or child support collection. Third, they discuss the seminal cost-benefit analysis that has been done in education, that of the Perry Preschool Program by Steven Barnett, and review four cost-effectiveness educational studies, as well as relevant literature from benefit-cost work in other fields.

Steven Barnett's goal was to measure the cost effectiveness of the Perry Preschool Program. Barnett was able to design an experimental study whereby 3- and 4-year-old Black children were randomly assigned either to a preschool program or to a control group with no program. The study followed five waves of children totaling 123 over 4 years, 58 children in the experimental program and 65 in control groups. Barnett tracked the children through age 19. He compared the costs and benefits for each group including program costs, child care, all education, delinquency and crime, earnings and employment, and welfare. He found a positive net present value of benefits and costs, indicating that the preschool program achieved a positive social investment of up to seven dollars for every taxpayer dollar spent on early education.

In a later study Barnett assisted Leonard Masse with a similar experimental design to estimate the long-term return on investment of the Abecedarian preschool program that was started in North Carolina in the early 1970s.[18] Masse and Barnett isolated the costs of the special services offered to the children in high-quality programs and concluded that the average annual cost of the Abecedarian program was about $13,000 per child in 2002 dollars, or about twice the cost of the average Head Start program. Yet even at that high cost, by the time the preschoolers had reached age 21, the benefits outweighed the costs by a factor of four dollars for every dollar spent. Since the study was conducted in a middle-class area, the authors speculated that the payoff would probably be even greater in other communities, especially high-crime and low-income neighborhoods such as that of the Perry Preschool Project. Both the Perry and the Abecedarian studies are significant for their longitudinal nature and their experimental design. The Abecedarian study is important because it is a comprehensive program whose costs appear prohibitive. However, when long-term benefits are weighed against those initial high costs, the program is seen to provide a significant return on society's original investment.

Clive Belfield examined the rate of return to individuals, funders, program providers, and society in general of the Big Brothers Big Sisters (BBBS) mentoring program.[19] BBBS pairs adults with youths from single-parent families, where the adult takes on the role of sibling for the young person. Again, this study used an experimental design, with random assignment to the mentoring program or to nonparticipation. Previous researchers had found that BBBS participants were significantly less likely to engage in antisocial activities, had higher test scores, were more engaged at school, and reported enhanced peer and family relationships.[20] These findings led the authors to conclude that the BBBS program was "a strong and sensible investment."[21] However, none of the outcomes was expressed in economic terms or compared to the program costs. Absent the financial information, Belfield points out, the other study's conclusion was unwarranted. He then undertook to assign monetary values to the benefits the previous researchers had recorded and compare them to the costs of the program, defined as the costs incurred by the individual mentors plus the resource use by the funding agency. Belfield triangulated the results from three different approaches to the economic analysis of the program costs and benefits, and calculated the rate of return for BBBS participants and for society. His conclusion was that the societal rate of return was high, but the participant rate of return somewhat lower, leading him to predict that there would be limited program expansion.

The most sophisticated benefit-cost analyses in education are these studies of early childhood services. As with comprehensive mentoring programs for beginning teachers, such programs appear costly, although comparisons with other educational programs can be misleading since the methods for calculating costs may vary and different program characteristics may be included in the analyses. For example, costs may be calculated by averaging the expenditures by a funding source, or by the market prices paid by consumers, or by using the actual costs of delivering the program. Even these more rigorous studies have not taken into account all of the outcomes that might influence the benefit-cost ratios. The Perry Preschool studies, for example, did not consider effects on caregivers' education, parenting skills, well-being, and health.[22] Nonetheless, these careful studies demonstrate the gains, both for children and society, that result from preschool programs, and point the way for similar studies to be conducted in other areas of education, while at the same time suggesting a methodology with which to do them.

THE COSTS OF ATTRITION AND TURNOVER

As I showed in Chapter 3, large numbers of teachers leave the profession or move to other schools each year in addition to those who retire. The departure of teachers comes at a cost to schools and districts who must shell out money to recruit, interview, hire, and, to some extent, retrain replacements. This fact has attracted the attention of a number of researchers who have attempted to assess the cost of such teacher churning.

Most studies have used some kind of estimate to calculate costs, even if they are using real information about teacher turnover. The simplest approach is to use a percentage of an employee's salary plus benefits. A more complex model would include separation costs, replacement costs, and training costs, and to be fully comprehensive, might add a category to include the performance differential between the employee who leaves and the replacement, as well as accounting for vacancy costs, to reflect the added costs/savings realized while the position is still unfilled.[23]

The first recent teacher turnover cost analysis was performed in Texas.[24] The authors reviewed reports from industrial and business settings in order to arrive at a cost estimate in the form of a percentage of the leaving teacher's salary. They used two estimates, one conservative (25% of a leaver's salary plus benefits) and one "pragmatic" (150% of a leaver's salary) to assess turnover costs in five districts, based on their actual retention statistics. They retrieved additional information regarding separation, replacement, and training costs from three districts and added that to the mix. Using the most conservative turnover cost estimation method, they figured that Texas was losing approximately $329 million each year due to teacher turnover (with an average of $11,120 per teacher). The more liberal estimation suggested that costs ran up to $2.1 billion per year ($56,115 per teacher). The main problem with this very broad ranging calculation is that the formula is based on industrial models of turnover costs, not on actual data derived from schools. The ACORN project did the same kind of calculation for 64 Chicago neighborhood elementary schools and found the range to be from $10,329 to $77,470 per teacher, totaling $5,629,523 to $42,221,422 across all the schools.[25] The same criticisms apply to this study, and the huge range in estimates makes it difficult to act on the information.

Three researchers from Florida Atlantic University presented a paper at an international meeting in which they reported a study to compare two Florida school districts with regard to their actual costs of separation, replacement, and training.[26] In the smaller district they calculated the per-teacher turnover costs at $4,631 and in the larger district at $12,652. Their main point was that one should not assume that these costs are similar across all districts, and that actual cost data should be collected rather than relying on an estimate, which is likely to be wrong for any given district. Of interest to those concerned with the induction of new teachers is the fact that the larger district with the high per-teacher turnover cost had an attrition rate of 7.25% while the other district with the lower costs had more than twice the turnover rate at 16.4%. The larger district had invested heavily in its New Educator Support System (NESS),[27] that apparently was contributing to an increased retention rate while also increasing the per-teacher replacement cost.

The most recent attempt to look at actual expenses when assessing the cost of teacher turnover is to be found in a study conducted by consultants to the National Commission on Teaching and America's Future (NCTAF).[28] They surveyed five varied school districts, and collected data on eight different cost categories embracing direct expenditures such as advertising, recruiting, and hiring incentives, as well as items related to the proportional value of time spent by school or district administrators interviewing teacher candidates, doing outplacement, and so on. Some of these costs are incurred by the school, others at the district level. The eight cost categories comprised recruitment and advertising, the offer of special incentives such as signing bonuses, the administrative processing of new hires and costs associated with separation, training for new hires, training for first-time teachers (including induction programs), training for all teachers, "learning curve" (defined as the cost to student learning of having a less experienced teacher), and finally the transfer costs of changing a teacher to a new school.

They found that it was possible to make the desired calculations, but difficult because districts did not always have adequate systems in place for tracking the costs. The five districts, of varying size and demographics, had turnover rates ranging from 15.5% to 42.9% for the target year of 2002–03. In all cases there were more leavers than movers. With regard to calculating the costs of teacher turnover, the authors were hampered by the fact that not all the districts were able to provide them with a complete set of necessary data. The district with the best reporting record showed total turnover costs of $9,875, well in the range of that found by Shockley and colleagues in Florida. In the largest district (Chicago Public Schools) the cost per leaver was $17,872; in a small rural district the per-leaver cost was $4,366.

Thus numbers varied according to the peculiarities of the district under study. Even acknowledging the lack of complete data for all districts, we are clearly going to find wide divergence in turnover costs from setting to setting, with the biggest costs found in the largest urban districts. Per-teacher turnover cost, however, is not, in itself an indicator of district health. For example, a district that invests a large amount in recruitment and retention of teachers, as with a comprehensive induction program, may record a high per-teacher turnover cost, but have a low turnover rate. A district with a high turnover rate may invest less in those activities and so record a lower per-teacher turnover cost. While the NCTAF report recommends that districts should invest in teacher induction programs in order to improve retention rates, their study does not distinguish the percentage of teacher departures that were due to retirement. Without this information, it is not possible to calculate accurately how much an investment in induction is likely to have on overall turnover costs. Also, the NCTAF analysis did not take into account the relative loss in productivity between the teacher who left and the replacement, nor did it account for any salary differences, often a savings when the replacement is a beginner.

A study of teacher turnover costs conducted by researchers for the School Finance Redesign Project at the University of Washington did include an estimate of loss of productivity and of net replacement difference, in addition to the other factors.[29] Loss of productivity was to have been represented by the differences in value-added achievement between the students of the leaving teacher and the replacement. Since the district under scrutiny did not have such data readily available, the authors were forced to estimate these differences using average effect sizes[30] from three other studies.[31] After performing their calculations using the available data and reasonable methods for estimating other costs, they found the biggest contributions to the price of teacher turnover to be training costs, costs of lost productivity, and salary savings when senior teachers leave. They concluded:

> While the costs of administering the separation and hiring systems are not negligible, it is the lost human capital and the related productivity loss that should be of most concern to policy makers. These results also suggest that the cost of turnover varies by the experience (and compensation) level of the teacher, with the most costly turnover being for experienced, but not highly senior teachers. In a decentralized system, the cost of turnover is also likely to vary substantially among schools, making an overall cost estimate less useful than one might like…. The costs estimated here are also substantially less than the "rule of thumb" of 1 or 1.5 times the leaving employee's annual salary.[32]

The important contribution of their study is the observation about the productivity loss associated with turnover. This suggests that any thorough benefit-cost analysis related to teacher retention and turnover should take that factor into account.

THE COSTS AND BENEFITS OF A COMPREHENSIVE INDUCTION PROGRAM FOR TEACHERS

I turn now to the study my colleagues and I did that I mentioned at the start of this chapter, namely the benefit-cost analysis of the NTC comprehensive induction program, as it was applied in one school district.[33] To do the study we needed three kinds of information: a description of the educational intervention (i.e., the NTC comprehensive induction program), a listing of program costs, and an estimation of program benefits. We set an arbitrary time parameter of 5 years for this evaluation without meaning to imply that the program's impact ends after the fifth year. In fact, from a sociological and public policy perspective, the benefits of the intervention may extend out to the entire career of the teacher and well into the earning years of students.

We obtained actual cost information from the local county office of education, from program leaders, from the school district budget office, and from the California Department of Education. We included all major and minor costs in the analysis, including salaries, indirect costs, facilities costs, equipment and materials, program inputs (such as room rental and substitute teachers), and client inputs (such as teachers' personal time). Total costs divided by the number of new teachers amounted to $6,605 per teacher. Of these costs, the district paid about 35%, the state about 56% (through the BTSA program), and the remaining 9% came from time inputs imposed on new teachers and site administrators as part of implementing the program.

Benefits and program effects were generated, where we were able to construct monetary estimates, using data we had previously collected regarding teacher retention,[34] student achievement,[35] mentor effectiveness, and the time saving to principals for having to monitor beginning teachers less. Using historical retention data from teachers who had been in the program, we compared these to published state and national data in order to estimate the benefits added by the comprehensive induction program. We analyzed the student test score data for all teachers in the district over 5 years, computing the value-added gains for new teachers and comparing them to those of experienced teachers who had not previously been in the program. This analysis demonstrated that first- and second-year teachers were as effective as fourth-year teachers on average, sans the induction program. By looking at the salary differential we could monetize this apparent benefit afforded by the induction program. We set out to create monetary estimates for the program benefits as they accrued to each constituent, including the student, the beginning teacher, the school district, the state, and society. By far the biggest benefit came, not from retention savings (17%), but from estimated salary savings due to the increase in new teacher effectiveness (47%). When each constituency is taken to account, the returns on time and program resources expended show that all four groups—students, new teachers, districts, and the state—all benefit from the investment in comprehensive induction. Students, who invest nothing, proportionally benefit the most, followed by new teachers who earn a return of $3.61, and the district which receives $1.88 per dollar invested. Even the state manages to recoup 98 cents on the dollar from its original investment. When costs and benefits are summed up for society, the program shows a return of $1.66 after 5 years for every dollar invested.

As we have seen, most discussions of induction benefits and costs focus on the savings from reduced turnover to justify program invest-ments.[36] By measuring the full range of benefit streams accruing to induction, we were able to demonstrate that induction returns appear to extend beyond mere retention questions. The influence on new-teacher practice is by far the most important benefit and potentially extends even farther if we consider the advantages to children assigned to effective teachers over the course of their K–12 careers. Of course our optimism over these findings must be tempered by the following facts: First, we only had data for one school district; second, we relied on value-added data to estimate teacher effectiveness benefits; third, we did not collect actual attrition costs, but estimated them using a percentage of a new teacher's salary.

ASSESSING THE EVIDENCE: ARE INDUCTION PROGRAMS COST-EFFECTIVE?

To be able to answer this question requires that one be in posses-sion of solid evidence regarding the relationship of induction support with teacher effectiveness and teacher retention. It is pretty clear that teacher turnover can be costly to a school or school district. There is also substantial evidence suggesting a correlation between induction programs and teacher retention such that one may legitimately hy-pothesize a savings of some degree from a reduction in loss of teachers to the profession. The connection between induction support and stu-dent achievement, as we have seen, is more tenuous. Where it can be demonstrated, an increase in teacher effectiveness may result in even more savings than a decrease in turnover. However, we continue to lack any definitive proof of the cost effectiveness of teacher induction programs, and need to be satisfied that one study of a comprehensive new teacher support program demonstrates that its benefits outweigh the costs over a 5-year period. It would be premature to generalize from a single study, but not to be optimistic that such programs have the potential to be a good investment of public funds.

Chapter 7

Conclusion:
Assessing the Evidence

Only since the middle of the 1990s have researchers started to investigate in earnest the effectiveness of induction and mentoring programs for new teachers. These researchers have studied several different outcomes. They have assessed the degree of satisfaction and polled the reflective opinions of new teachers and their mentors; they have studied the effects on teacher retention rates, student achievement gains, and teacher practice; and they have studied whether teacher induction programs are cost effective.

We have seen that induction and mentoring programs can take many forms, be comprised of few or many components, be state mandated or not, and be well funded or not. Induction programs usually include some form of mentoring, but this might vary from the mostly informal support of an available teacher colleague to formal support from a full-time visiting mentor who is trained and selected for that role. Recommendations that arise from research studies will need to take into account the specifics of the programs and settings under investigation, requiring the addition of restrictions and caveats to any generalizations about the potential effectiveness of induction for beginning teachers.

Not surprisingly, satisfaction studies find that, for the most part, teachers are satisfied.[1] Usually, teachers have no way of comparing the support they are actually receiving with what might be available under more optimal conditions, so they are pleased with whatever assistance they get. However, a group of Australian researchers led by Brian Hansford,[2] after reviewing 159 studies of educational mentoring, while emphasizing the generally positive perceptions of both teachers and mentors, draw our attention to a not inconsequential minority of studies that point to what his countrywoman Janette Long describes as the "dark side of mentoring."[3] For example, they cite one study where mentoring relationships created tensions that were exacerbated by political conflicts that emanated from the school district.[4] Other problems they find in their review of the research include mentors' complaints that mentoring took them away from their own classrooms only to spend time helping teachers with logistics and paperwork, and teachers complaining that their mentors were not knowledgeable about the latest teaching techniques, or that mentors were unsupportive and intrusive. Of all the studies they reviewed, a little over half reported some negative outcomes along with the positive, while four uncovered exclusively negative outcomes.

The following year, the same group of Australian authors furthered their effort to determine from the literature on mentoring to what extent it might be "a beneficial force in education."[5] In this report, the authors added to their review mentoring studies from the fields of business and medicine. They categorized the findings from the studies according to the kinds of benefits or problems reported, and elaborated further on the findings they had reported in the previous study. Mentored teachers most frequently stated that they were grateful for the emotional support, assistance with teaching, collegial discussions, and constructive criticism. Most common problems were lack of time for mentoring, mismatch of mentor and mentee, overly critical or out-of-touch mentors, and difficulties being observed. One should be careful, however, not to jump to the conclusion that mentoring beginning teachers is intrinsically fraught with problems. It is more likely that, when the outcomes were less than desirable, the program itself had some shortcomings. The authors state: "In many cases where mentoring programs were reported to have negative outcomes, program success appeared to have been jeopardized by lack of funding, lack of time, or poor matching of mentors and mentees."[6]

In a study from the early 1990s, Kip Tellez also suggested that formal mentoring may not always be a positive experience for beginning teachers.[7] He questioned 128 first-year teachers in Southern California and found that more than 25% were "generally dissatisfied" with their mentors. Overall, he found that the teachers in his study preferred to seek help from colleagues than from their assigned mentors,[8] leading him to conclude that informal mentoring was more important than formal mentoring. He did not check on the degree to which the formal mentoring program was well and faithfully implemented. Such findings, however, serve to remind us that mentoring may take many forms, and that we should not assume that assigning a mentor automatically results in the provision of the kind of support that new teachers find desirable. These studies notwithstanding, teachers usually speak favorably of induction support, however minimal it may be.

The efforts to measure the links between induction programs and new-teacher retention suggest that the more support there is the less likely are teachers to quit. However, as we saw in Chapter 3, the strength of this relationship and the confidence with which we can posit causality are both somewhat tenuous. Difficulty accessing reliable data, variations in definitions of retention, differences in the form of induction programs, and lack of information regarding the implementation of the described programs are factors that challenge our ability to draw conclusions. Furthermore, we are not clear on what a desirable retention rate might be, and whether the more effective teachers are the ones being retained.

Connections with teacher practice are even harder to determine, chiefly because of the difficulty in measuring and assessing the quality of teaching behavior. Of the few studies that have attempted to measure effects of induction on practice, most have used teacher self-reports as evidence of what they are doing in the classroom. Since self-report data are notoriously unreliable we are left with scant evidence of the effects of mentoring and induction on teacher practice, and the prospect that it may not even be possible to conduct a convincing study to link the two.

Challenges also exist in the quest to determine whether mentoring and induction may influence student learning. Again, researchers are faced with the problems of obtaining student test scores or other usable measures of student knowledge. Where these data exist, such as in the form of standardized test scores linked to teachers, most researchers adopt value-added modeling as the method of choice for measuring school or teacher effectiveness. Even when one rejects the many criticisms of this form of assessing effectiveness, it is rarely possible to set up an experimental study where hypotheses can be tested while controlling for the numerous other variables that can influence student achievement. The small number of studies that have been conducted point to the possible effect of comprehensive new teacher induction on student achievement, but these studies are not strong enough for us to draw any definitive conclusions.

Whether induction programs are worth the money invested in them depends, of course, on how effective they are in producing positive outcomes. The one study that suggests a 5-year return on investment is based on data from one of the most highly regarded programs in the country. The effectiveness data from this program are also subject to all the caveats already noted. Thus the indication of value for money must be qualified by our awareness of the shortcomings of nonexperimental research and the understanding that it is not possible to create the highest quality program in all settings.

What then can we say about the research on teacher induction? First, it is a nontrivial task to examine the effectiveness of new-teacher induction programs. Particularly complicated is the measurement and observation of teacher practice. Educators can learn a lot from psychologists and cognitive scientists about the evaluation of human behavior, and, up to now, they have mostly ignored or overlooked the evidence from those fields. Second, while most published findings, though few, are positive, taken as a whole they provide us only with thin evidence of the effectiveness of induction and mentoring. Lack of access to data, the paucity of opportunities and resources for conducting true experiments, and the diversity of contexts and forms of induction support restrict our ability to draw firm conclusions.

In short, we are not clear how effective induction is. The evidence is by no means overwhelming that induction and mentoring programs influence more than teachers' sense of well-being and their rates of attrition, and is very scant on the outcomes of student achievement and teacher practice. Future researchers need to find funding to conduct well-designed, experimental studies that focus on student achievement, and to develop a reliable method for observing and evaluating teacher practice in the classroom. In the meantime, we can console ourselves with the knowledge that the evidence that does exist suggests to us that, where comprehensive programs are established and funded, excellent teachers like Kesner Ridge will not quit before they finish their second year.

Notes

Chapter 1

1. Polly Curtis, "Why an award-winning young teacher wants to quit," *Guardian Unlimited*, January 7, 2003.

2. NCTAF, 2003.

3. Hargreaves & Fullan, 2000.

4. The Schools and Staffing Survey (SASS), is administered by the National Center for Education Statistics (NCES). To date, six independent cycles of SASS have been completed: 1987–88, 1990–91, 1993–94, 1999–2000, 2003–04, and 2007–08.

5. Smith & Ingersoll, 2004.

6. Feiman-Nemser, Carver, Schwille, & Yusko, 1999.

7. NCLB requirements for those who are new to the profession (less than one year of experience):

- The procedure for demonstrating subject matter knowledge depends on a teacher's tenure and level of instruction.
- Elementary teachers must pass a state test demonstrating their subject knowledge and teaching skills in reading/language arts, writing, mathematics, and other areas of basic elementary school curricula.
- Middle and high school teachers must demonstrate a high level of competency in each academic subject area they teach. Such demonstration can occur either through passage of a rigorous state academic subject test or successful completion of an undergraduate major, a graduate degree, coursework equivalent to an undergraduate major, or an advanced certification or credentialing.
- Experienced teachers can satisfy the subject matter requirement in the same manner as new teachers or demonstrate subject knowledge through a state-determined high objective uniform state standard of evaluation (HOUSSE).

These requirements have caused some difficulty in implementation especially for special education teachers and teachers in small rural schools who are often called upon to teach multiple grades and subjects.

Chapter 2

1. Jennings, 1971.
2. Roche, 1979.
3. Allen, Eby, Poteet, Lentz, & Lima, 2004.
4. Kram, 1985.
5. E.g., Ensher & Murphy, 1997; Noe, 1988; Scandura, 1992; Scandura & Viator, 1994; Tepper, Shaffer, & Tepper, 1996.
6. Zey, 1984.
7. Ashburn, 1987; Association of Teacher Educators, 1989; Huling-Austin, 1989; Theis-Sprinthall, 1986.
8. Bowers & Eberhart, 1988; Gehrke & Kay, 1984; Henry, 1989; Littleton, Tally-Foos, & Wolaver, 1992.
9. Berliner, 1986.
10. Furtwengler, 1995.
11. "Quality Counts 2008," 2008.
12. Smith & Ingersoll, 2004.
13. E.g., Britton & Paine, 2005.
14. From the NTC Web site at http://newteachercenter.org/ti_scsvntp.php
15. From the BTSA Web site at http://www.btsa.ca.gov/
16. CCTE, 2002.
17. According to CCTE & CDE, 1997, these standards are organized around six interrelated categories of teaching practice:

- Engaging and supporting all students in learning
- Creating and maintaining effective environments for student learning
- Understanding and organizing subject matter for student learning
- Planning instruction and designing learning experiences for all students
- Assessing student learning
- Developing as a professional educator

18. From the BTSA Web site at www.btsa.ca.gov/fact
19. Connecticut State Department of Education (Bureau of Educator Preparation, Certification, Support and Assessment), 2007–2008.
20. NCTAF, 2005.
21. Costa & Garmston, 1994.
22. Goldstein, 2007.
23. Yusko & Feiman-Nemser, 2008.
24. Goldstein, 2007.
25. Goldstein, 2004.
26. Britton, Paine, Pimm, & Raizen, 2003; Wong, Britton, & Ganzer, 2005.

27. Moskowitz & Stephens, 1997.
28. E.g., Tickle, 2000.
29. Eisenschmidt, 2006.
30. Stoel & Thant, 2002.
31. Veenman & Denessen, 2001.
32. Lazovsky & Reichenberg, 2006.
33. Wong et al., 2005.
34. Britton et al., 2003.
35. Moskowitz & Stephens, 1997.
36. Wang & Odell, 2007.
37. Feiman-Nemser, 2001; quote from p. 18.
38. Feiman-Nemser, 2001, p. 28.
39. Athanases & Achinstein, 2003.
40. Achinstein & Barrett, 2004.
41. E.g., Kagan, 1992.
42. Strong & Baron, 2004.
43. Wang, Strong, & Odell, 2004.
44. Luft & Cox, 2001.
45. Hall, Johnson, & Bowman, 1995.
46. Moran, Dallat, & Abbot, 1999; Oberski, Ford, Higgins, & Fisher, 1999.
47. Most teachers are not in a position to discern differences among alternative forms of support, so they tend to express satisfaction with whatever they are offered, since it is likely to be better than nothing at all.

Chapter 3

1. Marlow, Inman, & Betancourt-Smith, 1997.
2. E.g., Ingersoll, 2001, 2002; Ingersoll & Kralik, 2004.
3. E.g., Bobbitt, Faupel, & Burns, 1991; Bobbitt, Leich, Whitener, & Lynch, 1994.
4. Boe, Bobbitt, & Cook, 1997.
5. Robinson & Smithers, 1991; Smithers & Robinson, 2002.
6. E.g., Scafidi, Sjoquist, & Stinebrickner, 2007; Hanushek, Kain, & Rivkin, 2001.
7. Hanushek et al., 2001.
8. Provasnik & Dorfman, 2005, pp. 2–3.
9. Henke, Chen, Geis, & Knepper, 2000; Provasnik & Dorfman, 2005.
10. Flyer & Rosen, 1997.
11. Broughman & Rollefson, 2000.
12. U.S. Department of Education, National Center for Education Statistics, 2005.
13. U.S. Census Bureau, 2005; Provasnik & Dorfman, 2005.
14. Broughman & Rollefson, 2000.
15. Strizek, Pittsonberger, Riordan, Lyter, & Orlofsky, 2006.
16. Gordon, 1994.

17. E.g., Dupre, 1986; Robinson, 1981.

18. Guarino, Santibañez, & Daley, 2006.

19. Green & Weaver, 1992; Hood & Parker, 1994.

20. E.g., Corcoran, Evans, & Schwab, 2004; Hanushek & Pace, 1995; Temin, 2002.

21. Ballou, 1996; Ehrenberg & Brewer, 1994, 1995; Ferguson, 1991; Ferguson & Ladd, 1996; Mosteller & Moynihan, 1972.

22. E.g., Henke et al., 2000; Gitomer, Latham, & Ziomek, 1999; Podgursky, Monroe, & Watson, 2004.

23. Henke et al., 2000.

24. College quality is defined according to Barron's *Profiles of American Colleges*, 1991, which ranks colleges according to the selectiveness of their admissions policies.

25. Ballou, 1996.

26. E.g., Cochran-Smith, 2004; Farkas, Johnson, & Foleno, 2000; Nieto, 2005.

27. Provasnik & Dorfman, 2005, pp. 23–24.

28. E.g., Hanushek, Kain, & Rivkin, 2004; Ingersoll, 2001; Kirby, Berends, & Nafitel, 1999; Murnane & Olsen, 1990.

29. Liu, 2007, p. 13.

30. Shen & Palmer, 2005.

31. Henke et al., 2000.

32. Reed, Reuben, & Barbou, 2006.

33. E.g., Gritz & Theobald, 1996; Ingersoll, 2001; Kirby et al., 1999.

34. E.g., Kirby, Grissmer, & Hudson, 1991; Murnane, Singer, & Willet, 1989.

35. Ingersoll, 2001; Kirby et al., 1999.

36. Quartz et al., 2008.

37. E.g. Henke et al., 2000; Lankford, Loeb, & Wyckoff, 2002; Podgursky et al., 2004.

38. E.g., Grissmer & Kirby, 1997; Stinebrickner, 2002.

39. Murnane & Olsen, 1990.

40. Murnane & Schwinden, 1989.

41. Goldhaber, Gross, & Player, 2007.

42. Henke & Zahn, 2001; Ingersoll, 2001; Stinebrickner, 2002.

43. Harris & Adams, 2007.

44. Henke & Zahn, 2001.

45. Ingersoll, 2003.

46. Stinebrickner, 2002.

47. Harris & Adams, 2007.

48. Provasnik & Dorfman, 2005, p. 24.

49. Connolly, 2000; Darling-Hammond, 2001; Grissmer & Kirby, 1997; Ingersoll, 1997; Murnane & Olsen, 1989, 1990; Olson, 2000; Scherer, 2001; Shen, 1997.

50. Bobbit, Faupel, & Burns, 1991; Connolly, 2000; Darling-Hammond, 2001; Harmon, 2001; Marlow et al., 1997; Olson, 2000.

51. Darling-Hammond, 2001; Marlow et al., 1997.

52. Connolly, 2000; Darling-Hammond, 2001; Marlow et al., 1997.

53. Connolly, 2000; Darling-Hammond, 2001; Merseth, 1992.

54. Grissmer & Kirby, 1997; Ingersoll, 1997; Murnane & Olsen, 1989, 1990.

55. Boe, Bobbit, & Cook, 1997; Grissmer & Kirby, 1997; Lucksinger, 2000; Murnane & Olsen, 1989, 1990.

56. Grissmer & Kirby, 1992; Murnane & Olsen, 1989, 1990.

57. Grissmer & Kirby, 1992; Murnane & Olsen, 1989, 1990.

58. Harmon, 2001.

59. Connolly, 2000; Jones & Sandidge, 1997.

60. Jones & Sandidge, 1997; Shen, 1997.

61. Connolly, 2000; Jones & Sandidge, 1997.

62. Darling-Hammond, 2001; Theobald, 1990.

63. Bacharach, Bamberger, Conley, & Bauer, 1990; Darling-Hammond & Wise, 1983; Ingersoll, 1997; Scherer, 2001.

64. Connolly, 2000; Darling-Hammond, 2001; Grissmer & Kirby, 1997; Murphy, 1993; Shen, 1997.

65. Darling-Hammond, 2001; Grissmer & Kirby, 1997; Murphy, 1993; Shen, 1997.

66. Murnane & Olsen, 1989, 1990.

67. Dolton & Van der Klaauw, 1995, 1999.

68. Theobald & Gritz, 1996.

69. Kirby & Grissmer, 1993; Grissmer & Kirby, 1997.

70. Harris & Adams, 2007.

71. Stinebrickner, 1998.

72. The proportional hazards model, proposed by Cox, 1972, has been used primarily in medical testing analysis, to model the effect of secondary variables on survival. It is a regression model that assumes hazard rate is a function of the independent variables (covariates). In this example, the covariate of a 25% increase in salary has a durative effect on a teacher's career, such that the hazard rate of quitting is reduced by 50%.

73. Stinebrickner, 2001.

74. Imazeki, 2002.

75. Ballou & Podgursky, 1998.

76. Hanushek et al., 2001.

77. Falch & Strøm, 2002.

78. Mont & Rees, 1996.

79. Latham & Vogt, 2007.

80. Ingersoll, 2003.

81. Ingersoll, 2001, 2003.

82. Liu, 2007, p.13.

83. Shen, 1997.

84. Hanushek, 2001.

85. Heyns, 1988; Theobald, 1990.

86. Kyriacou, 1989, 2001.

87. Cox & Griffiths, 1995.

88. Rosenholtz & Simpson, 1990.

89. Wisniewski & Gargiulo, 1997; Billingsley, 1993.

90. Rosenberg, Griffin, Kilgore, & Carpenter, 1997.

91. E.g., Billingsley, 1993; Bobbitt et al., 1991; Boe, Cook, Kaufman, & Danielson, 1995.

92. Billingsley & Cross, 1992; Stempien & Loeb, 2002.

93. Zabel & Zabel, 2001.

94. Billingsley, 2004.

95. Path analysis is an extension of the regression model and is used to test the fit of the correlation matrix against two or more causal models which are being compared by the researcher.

96. Gersten, Keating, Yobanoff, & Harniss, 2001.

97. Darling-Hammond, 2000.

98. Haberman, 1999, 2001.

99. Nieto, 2005, p. 7.

100. Johnson & Project on the Next Generation of Teachers, 2004.

101. Quartz et al., 2008.

102. Kirby & Grissmer, 1993.

103. Theobald, 1990, quote from p. 243.

104. Chapman, 1984, p. 657.

105. Chapman & Green, 1986, p. 277.

106. Ingersoll, 2001, 2002, 2003; Smith & Ingersoll, 2004.

107. Ingersoll, 2001, p. 19.

108. Shen, 1997.

109. E.g., Blair-Larsen, 1998; Feiman-Nemser & Parker, 1992; Fideler & Haselkorn, 1999; Ganser, 2002, 2005; Hargreaves & Fullan, 2000; Kelley, 2004; Schaffer, Stringfield, & Wolfe, 1992; Scherer, 1999; Villani, 2002; Wollman-Bonilla, 1997.

110. Some of the content of this section appeared in a slightly different form in Strong, 2005.

111. Ingersoll & Kralik, 2004.

112. Brown & Wambach, 1987; Cheng & Brown, 1992; Eberhard, Reinhardt-Mondragon, & Stottlemeyer, 2000.

113. Gold, 1987; Henke et al., 2000.

114. Spuhler & Zetler, 1995.

115. Ingersoll, 2000, 2001; Ingersoll, Alsalam, Quinn, & Bobbit, 1997; Ingersoll & Smith, 2003.

116. Odell & Ferraro, 1992.

117. Fuller, 2003; Charles A. Dana Center, 2002.

118. Smith & Ingersoll, 2004.

119. Ingersoll, 2001.

120. Smith & Ingersoll, 2004.

121. Shen, 1997.

122. Odell & Ferraro, 1992.

123. Fuller, 2003; Charles A. Dana Center, 2002.

124. Grant, 2004.

125. CCTC, 2002.

126. Riggs & Scott, 1999.
127. Scott-Hendrick & Childress, 2002; Spencer, 2000.
128. Strong & St. John, 2001.
129. CCTE, 2002.
130. Reed et al., 2006.
131. Youngs, 2002.
132. Elmore, 2003.
133. Rockoff, 2008.
134. Kapadia, Coca, & Easton, 2007.

Chapter 4

1. E.g., Goldhaber 2002; Goldhaber et al., 1999; Hanushek et al., 1999; Wright, Horn, & Sanders, 1997.
2. Cochran-Smith Fries, 2001.
3. Coleman et al., 1966. Note, however, that some researchers found fault with the design of the Coleman study, to the extent that its methodological shortcomings made it possible to draw few policy conclusions; see, e.g., Cain & Watts, 1970; Hanushek & Kain, 1972.
4. Value-added modeling (VAM) refers to a collection of statistical techniques that uses multiple years of student test score data to estimate the effects of individual schools or teachers on student achievement. Value-added models have two key features. First, the dependent variables in the analysis are designed to measure the amount of change that occurs in students' achievement during the year when students are in the classrooms under study. Second, measures of change are adjusted for differences across classrooms in students' prior achievement, home and social background (in some versions), and the social composition of the schools that students attend. The purpose of value-added models is to estimate the proportions of variance in changes in student achievement attributable to classrooms (i.e., teachers), after controlling for the effects of other, confounding variables. See Chapter 5 for a more detailed discussion of VAM.
5. Goldhaber, 2002; Goldhaber & Brewer, 2000; Hanushek, 1986, 1997.
6. Goldhaber, 2002.
7. Goldhaber, 2002, p. 53.
8. There is a difference between licensure and certification. Many professions such as law and medicine require a license in order to practice. The goal of licensing tests is to set a minimum level of competency, and to practice without a license is illegal. Teachers without certification are not allowed to use the title of "certified teacher" but are free to practice. This difference between certification and licensure allows states to issue emergency certificates but not emergency licenses.
9. The National Teachers Exam consisted of a single multiple-choice test of general knowledge and knowledge about teaching. Thirty states used the test in issuing provisional teaching certificates. It received much criticism, especially from teacher unions, for being overly simplistic, and was replaced in

the early 1990s by the *Praxis* series, which includes tests of subject-matter as well as pedagogical knowledge.

10. Strauss & Sawyer, 1986.

11. Harris & Sass, 2007.

12. Rice, 2003.

13. Darling-Hammond, 2002.

14. Goldhaber & Brewer, 2000.

15. E.g., Kane, Rockoff, & Staiger, 2006.

16. Hanushek, 1992.

17. Aaronson, Barrow, & Sander, 2007.

18. Rivkin, Hanushek, & Kain, 2005.

19. Sanders, 2000, p. 335.

20. Nye, Konstantopoulos, & Hedges, 2004.

21. Goldhaber & Anthony, 2007, p. 134.

22. Delandshere, 1994.

23. Stodolsky, 1990.

24. Fenstermacher & Richardson (2005).

25. According to Duncan & Biddle, 1974, *process* variables may be defined as properties of the interactive phase of instruction, i.e., the phase of instruction during which students and teachers interact around academic content. *Product* variables are the possible outcomes of teaching, including student achievement. In addition there are *presage* variables, defined as properties of teachers that can be assumed to operate prior to, but also to have an influence on, the interactive phase of teaching, and *context* variables, those that can exercise direct effects on instructional outcomes, condition the effects of process variables on product variables, or both.

26. Constructivism is a philosophical approach to learning, which argues that humans construct meaning from current knowledge.

27. Fenstermacher & Richardson, 2005, p. 209.

28. Most current definitions of teacher competence from which assessments follow, are the product of three organizations: the National Board for Professional Teacher Standards (NBPTS), the Interstate New Teacher Assessment Support Consortium (INTASC) and the National Council for Accreditation of Teacher Education (NCATE). . . . The three organizations acknowledge that teachers' actions or performances depend on many different kinds of knowledge as well as the dispositions to use that knowledge. They also recognize that teachers must work with others to support the learning and success of all students. The standards of competence described by the three organizations relate to a teacher's commitment to students and their students' learning, requiring that teachers

- should act on the belief that all students can learn
- should have deep subject matter knowledge about the substance and structure of their disciplines
- need to manage and monitor student learning, identify learning goals and choose from teaching styles to meet these goals

- need to be reflective about their teaching, and evaluate their decisions and experiences to make adjustments in their teaching
- must be part of a larger community consisting of school staff, parents, and the broader nonparent community

As the National Research Council notes, the standards currently in use ". . . illustrate the wide range of knowledge, skills, abilities, and dispositions that contemporary educators believe competent teachers must possess and demonstrate in the classroom" (Mitchell, Robinson, Plake, & Knowles, 2001, p. 31)," from Laczko-Kerr & Berliner, 2002.

29. Mitchell et al., 2001.
30. Reynolds, 1992.
31. Clark & Peterson, 1986.
32. E.g., Brophy & Good, 1986.
33. Simon & Boyer, 1974.
34. Lavely, Berger, Blackman, Follman, & McCarthy, 1994.
35. Flanders, 1970.
36. E.g., Flanders, 1970; LaShier, 1967; Rosenshine & Furst, 1973.
37. E.g., Hughes, 1970; Townsend, 1976.
38. Medley & Mitzel, 1958, p. 91.
39. Teddlie, Kirby, & Stringfield, 1989.
40. Teddlie et al., 1989, p. 222.
41. Rosenshine, 1983, p. 337.
42. Saldana & Waxman, 1997.
43. Danielson & McGreal, 2000.
44. Danielson, 2007.
45. Danielson, 2007, p. 66.
46. E.g., Gallagher, 2004; Kimball, White, Milanowski, 2004; Milanowski, 2004.
47. HLM is particularly well suited for such analyses because it takes into account the nested nature of the data in which students are situated within classrooms and classrooms within schools. With HLM, variation in student achievement can be explained as a function of classroom and/or school characteristics while still taking into account variance within classrooms or schools at the student level. It can also estimate between- and within-group (e.g., within and between classrooms)variance at the same time, making for more precise estimates of school and classroom effects (Arnold, 1992; Raudenbush & Bryk, 2002). For statistically minded readers the conventional value-added HLM model can be shown as follows (Meyer, 1996):

$$\text{Posttest}_{ics} = \gamma + \theta\text{Pretest}_{ics} + \alpha\text{StudChar}_{ics} + \pi_{cs} + \varepsilon_{ics},$$

where γ is a constant, θ and α are model parameters for student pretest scores and student/family characteristics, π is the teacher effect to be estimated, ε captures the unobserved student-level determinants, i indexes individual students, c indexes teachers, and s indexes schools.

48. Peterson, 2000, p. ix.

49. Medley & Coker, 1987, p.243.

50. Medley & Coker, 1987, found correlations between principal performance ratings and learning gains of 0.10 to 0.23.

51. E.g., Peterson, 1987, 2000.

52. Jacob & Lefgren, 2008.

53. Wason, 1960.

54. Francis Bacon, 1621/1902, said: "The human understanding, when any proposition has been once laid down. . . ., forces everything else to add fresh support and confirmation: and although most cogent and abundant instances may exist to the contrary, yet either does not observe, or despises them, or it gets rid of and rejects them by some distinction, with violent and injurious prejudice, rather than sacrifice the authority of its first conclusions" (Aphorism XLVI, p. 23 of the 1902 edition).

55. E.g., Wason, 1971; Wason & Johnson-Laird, 1968.

56. E.g., Mynatt, Doherty, & Tweney, 1977; Nickerson, 1998; Edwards & Smith, 1996.

57. Kunda, 1990.

58. Mack & Rock, 1998.

59. Simons & Chabris, 1999; after an original experiment by Becklen & Cervone, 1983.

60. Simons, 2000.

61. Video clips of this stunt can be found on YouTube at http://www.youtube.com/watch?v=UYeJ1BHHDIg

62. Miller, 1956.

63. Simon, 1957.

64. Gregory, 1980.

65. Gregory, 1997.

66. Desecribed in Kahneman, 2002.

67. Bruner & Postman, 1949.

68. Bruner & Postman, 1949, p. 168.

69. Bruner & Potter, 1964.

70. Ross, Lepper, & Hubbard, 1975.

71. E.g., Davis, Lohse, & Kottemann, 1994, had MBA students from an advanced finance course forecast stock earnings using a computerized information system designed to simulate systems used in practice. Disguised actual company data were presented in three different treatments: baseline information, baseline plus redundant news information, and baseline plus nonredundant news information. The redundant information made subjects significantly more confident in their forecasts compared to the baseline case. The nonredundant information made subjects significantly more confident than both the baseline case and the redundant case. Forecast accuracy, however, was significantly diminished in both the redundant and nonredundant conditions compared to baseline. Thus, the additional news information, whether redundant or nonredundant, had the effect of degrading performance while increasing confidence. The authors concluded that decision makers may be poor judges of the usefulness of newly available information sources, and may be

influenced by information that does not improve their performance under the false impression that it is helpful. I also had experiences with belief perseverance during a study of children's reading comprehension when I was a graduate student at UC Berkeley. We showed children short stories by revealing the text a sentence or two at a time. After they saw the first presentation the children were asked to guess what they thought the story was about. They held on to their original hypotheses long after subsequent revelations of text proved that their earlier guesses were way off.

72. E.g., Christensen-Szalanski, 1991; Fischhoff, 2001; Hawkins & Hastie, 1990.

73. Christensen-Szalanski, 1991; Fischhoff, 2001; Fischhoff & Beyth, 1975; Hawkins & Hastie, 1990; Slovic & Fischhoff, 1977.

74. E.g., James, 1890/1950; Johnson-Laird, 1983; Neisser, 1963; Piaget, 1926; Vygotsky, 1934/1987.

75. E.g., Chaiken and Trope, 1999; Epstein, 1994; Kahneman & Frederick, 2002; Sloman, 1996.

76. Stanovich & West, 2000.

77. Gladwell, 2005.

78. Frederick, 2005.

79. Frederick, 2005, p 27.

80. Kahneman, 2002.

81. Wang, Odell, & Schwille, 2008. Some of the studies they review are discussed in Chapter 6.

82. ERIC stands for Education Resources Information Center, a resource sponsored by the U.S. Department of Education, Institute of Education Sciences (IES). It provides free access to more than 1.2 million bibliographic records of journal articles and other education-related materials and, if available, includes links to full text.

83. Wang et al., 2008, p. 134.

84. Wang et al., 2008, p. 134.

85. Evertson & Smithey, 2000.

86. Wang et al., 2008, p. 147.

87. Roehrig, Bohn, Turner, & Pressley, 2008.

88. Roehrig et al., 2008, p. 693.

89. Thompson et al., 2004a.

90. A quasi-experimental design is one that looks a bit like an experimental design but lacks the key ingredient—random assignment. With respect to internal validity, quasi experiments often appear to be inferior to randomized experiments. Since one has not randomly assigned subjects to groups, one cannot assume that the populations being compared are equivalent on all things prior to the treatment, and accordingly internal validity is threatened. When a posttreatment difference between groups is observed, one cannot with great confidence attribute that effect to the treatment, since the groups may have had preexisting differences that caused the observed posttreatment difference.

91. Their model included four aspects of teaching that were theorized to lead to student engagement in the learning process: (1) learning environment (safety, inclusiveness, and procedures that support learning); (2) facilitation of

learning, (questioning, feedback, learning activities, and differentiation for different learners); (3) quality of the learning goals (appropriateness, depth, and degree of challenge); and (4) representation of content (accuracy, depth, connections, and scaffolding). Generally, these were aspects of teaching that could be observed as actions or behaviors of the teacher or features of the classroom environment.

92. Thompson, Paek, Goe, & Ponte, 2004c, p. 4.

Chapter 5

1. "Under No Child Left Behind, each state has developed and implemented measurements for determining whether its schools and local educational agencies (LEAs) are making adequate yearly progress (AYP). AYP is an individual state's measure of progress toward the goal of 100 percent of students achieving to state academic standards in at least reading/language arts and math. It sets the minimum level of proficiency that the state, its school districts, and schools must achieve each year on annual tests and related academic indicators. Parents whose children are attending Title I (low-income) schools that do not make AYP over a period of years are given options to transfer their child to another school or obtain free tutoring (supplemental educational services)."

From the U. S. Department of Education Web site at http://answers.ed.gov and selecting "Adequate yearly progress." The problem with this measure is that it is affected by the performance levels of the entering students. Those at a higher level will have little difficulty reaching AYP. If the new student cohorts vary from year to year, schools sometimes may have difficulty reaching their desired targets, for reasons that have nothing to do with the quality of the school.

2. E.g., Swanson, 2003.

3. Wong, 2004.

4. E.g., Matsumura, Garnier, Pascal, & Valdes, 2002.

5. Ballou, 2002.

6. Braun, 1988.

7. Rothstein, 2007, 2008.

8. McCaffrey, Lockwood, Koretz, & Hamilton, 2003; McCaffrey, Lockwood, Koretz, Louis, & Hamilton, 2004.

9. William Sanders is now in private business promoting the Education Value-Added Assessment System (EVAAS). EVAAS is a data analysis and reporting service offered by SAS in Schools, a private company in North Carolina. SAS in Schools analyzes test scores and provides schools and school districts with information about the value added to each student's knowledge and skills by each teacher in the school or district who instructs students in areas that are assessed by standardized achievement tests.

10. Sanders, Saxton, & Horn, 1997.

11. E.g., Sanders, 2000, p. 334.

12. E.g., Ballou, 2002; Kupermintz, 2003.

13. Sanders & Horn, 1998, p. 251.

14. Ballou, Sanders, & Wright, 2004.

15. Kane & Staiger, 2002, p. 105.

16. Kupermintz, 2003.

17. Kupermintz, 2003, p. 289 (emphasis in original).

18. Amrein-Beardsley, 2008.

19. Sanders, Ashton, & Wright, 2005.

20. Amrein-Beardsley, 2008, p. 71.

21. Webster & Mendro, 1997.

22. Stephen W. Raudenbush, a professor of sociology and chair of the Committee on Education at the University of Chicago, quoted in Stewart, 2006.

23. Daniel Koretz of Harvard, quoted in Stewart, 2006.

24. Sanders, 2000, p. 335.

25. Hoff, 2007, cited in Amrein-Beardsley, 2008.

26. CAT-6, the *California Achievement Tests*, 6th ed., published by CTB McGraw-Hill, is the normative component of California's standardized assessment system, introduced in 2003 and successor to the *Stanford Achievement Test*, 9th ed. (SAT9). It was only administered to students taking the grades 3 and 7 tests in that year. It tests reading, language arts, spelling, and mathematics. The CAT-6 allows a comparison of California students against others from across the nation, and is intended to provide a snapshot of California students referenced against a national cross section. Its content reflects national standards and its results contribute to the Academic Performance Index (API).

27. CSTs were developed by California educators and test developers specifically for California. They are criterion-referenced tests that measure progress toward California's state-adopted academic content standards, which describe what students should know and be able to do in each grade and subject tested. Together with the CAT-6 and special education and Spanish language tests, they make up California's Standardized Testing and Reporting (STAR) program, administered by ETS.

28. See Chapter 4, note 46.

29. Thompson, Paek, Goe, & Ponte, 2004b, p. 13.

30. Fletcher, Strong & Villar, 2008; two studies are reported in this article.

31. See Chapter 4, note 89.

32. The normal curve equivalent (NCE) is a way of measuring where a student falls along the normal curve. The numbers on the NCE line run from 1 to 99, similar to percentile ranks, which indicate an individual student's rank, or how many students out of a hundred had a lower score. NCE scores have a major advantage over percentiles in that they can be averaged. That is an important characteristic when studying overall school performance, and in particular, in measuring schoolwide gains and losses in student achievement.

In a normally distributed population, if all students were to make exactly one year of progress after one year of instruction, then their NCE scores would remain exactly the same and their NCE gain would be zero, even though their raw scores (i.e., the number of questions they answered correctly) increased. Some students will make more than a year's progress in that time and will have a net gain in the NCE score, which means that those students have learned more, or at least have made more progress in the areas tested, than the general population. Other students, while making progress in their skills, may progress more slowly than the general population and will show a net loss in their NCE ranks. As with many other scales related to the normal curve, the average NCE, by definition, is 50. If all students improve in their performance, the mean, or NCE 50, will represent a higher raw score.

33. RCTs are most commonly seen in the medical field because of their ability to eliminate spurious causality and bias, but are also seen in other fields such as engineering, sociology, and, more recently, education. As the name suggests, RCTs involve the random allocation of different interventions (or treatments) to subjects, as well as the random selection of subjects. This ensures that known and unknown confounding factors are evenly distributed between or among treatment groups.

34. Glazerman, Senesky, Seftor, & Johnson, 2006.

35. As previously described by ETS on their Web site: The Pathwise Series offers a comprehensive array of professional development programs tied to research-based standards (i.e., those developed by Charlotte Danielson) to help teachers at all levels (student, beginning, and experienced) improve their teaching practices. The series consists of workshops, training sessions and related materials, and instructional minicourses, as well as Web-delivered professional development courses. Programs cover topics such as beginning-teacher induction, professional portfolio development, observation programs for formalizing evaluation, teacher evaluation system design, and training in professional skills for leaders. See www.greenlightforlearning.com.

36. The cluster assignment approach maintains the primary strength of random assignment—the provision of unbiased impact estimates—but has less statistical power than random assignment of individuals, which usually is not possible for programs focused on whole groups. MPR describes and defends this process in detail in a separate report: Schochet, 2005.

37. In October 2008, MPR released a report of the first-year findings from their randomized control study. They found no significant differences between the treatment and control groups in any of the main outcomes. While this may be initially surprising, it is actually not that unexpected, since the data were collected during or after only the first year of intervention, implementation of the treatment programs was imperfect in some sites, and 75% of the teachers in the control group had an assigned mentor, with a further 8% reporting having had the services of a mentor who was not formally assigned. Since the treatment programs typically specify a 2-year exposure and the control group may have had induction support that was not significantly different in many respects to that received by the treatment group, it would be unlikely to find significant differences in the outcome measures, even if implementation had been perfect. See Glazerman, Dolfin, Bleeker, Johnson, Isenberg, Lugo-Gil, Grider, & Britton, 2008.

38. Rockoff, 2008.

39. With certain kinds of nonexperimental data one can get much closer to the virtues of a randomized experiment by using a fixed effects model to control for all possible characteristics of the individuals in the study—even without measuring them—so long as those characteristics do not change over time. This is a powerful claim, and it often takes some justifying. If the dependent variable is quantitative, then fixed effects methods can be easily implemented using a procedure known as ordinary least squares linear regression. When the dependent variable is categorical, somewhat more sophisticated methods are necessary, but even then the fixed effects approach is a lot easier than many alternative methods. There are two key data requirements for the application of a fixed effects method. First, each individual in the sample must have two or more measurements on the same dependent variable. Second, for at least some of the individuals in the sample, the values of the independent variable(s) of interest must be different on at least two of the measurement occasions. Rothstein's problem with VAMs that use fixed effects estimators is that they don't live up to the standard of controlling for all possible characteristics of the individuals in the study.

40. Ross, 1992.

Chapter 6

1. Villar & Strong, 2007.
2. Gramlich, 1998.
3. This standard is named after Vilfredo Pareto, an Italian economist who used the concept in his studies of economic efficiency and income distribution.
4. This standard is named after Baron Nicholas Kaldor, a prominent Cambridge economist of the postwar period, and Sir John Hicks, an influential economist who received the Nobel Prize for economics in 1972 (with Kenneth Arrow).
5. E.g., Mishan, 1976.
6. Kelman, 1981; Nussbaum, 2001.
7. Solow, 1981.
8. Herrnstein, 1997.
9. Heaton & Throsby, 1998.
10. Lambur, Rajgopal, Lewis, Cox, & Ellerbrock, 2003.
11. Whalen & Wright, 1999.
12. Daneshvary & Clauretie, 2001.
13. Masse & Barnett, 2002.
14. Fuerst & Fuerst, 1993.
15. Barnett, 1985.
16. See Munoz & Munoz, 2000.
17. Hummel-Rossi & Ashdown, 2002.
18. Masse & Barnett, 2002.
19. Belfield, 2003.

20. Grossman & Tierney, 1998.

21. Grossman & Tierney, 1998, p. 423, quoted in Belfield, 2003, p. 7.

22. Fraser, 2003.

23. Pinkovitz, Moskal, & Schaefer, 1997.

24. Texas Center for Educational Research, 2000.

25. Association of Community Organizations for Reform Now (ACORN), 2004.

26. Shockley, Guglielmino, & Watlington, 2006.

27. NESS is described on the Broward County Public Schools Human Resource Development Web site (http://www.broward.K12.fl.us/HRD/teachers/ness.htm) as: "A site-based program to assist educators in developing effective teaching behaviors and to retain qualified teachers by connecting New Educators to a supportive system."

28. Barnes, Crowe, & Shaefer, 2007.

29. Milanowski & Odden, 2007.

30. An *effect size* is the percent of variance in the dependent variable that can be explained by the independent variable.

31. Clotfelter, Ladd, & Vigdor, 2006; Hanushek, Kin, O'Brien, & Rivkin, 2005; Kane et al., 2006.

32. Milanowski & Odden, 2007, p. 16.

33. Villar & Strong, 2007.

34. Strong & St. John, 2001.

35. Strong et al., 2008.

36. Barnes et al., 2007; Fuller, 2003; Milanowski & Odden, 2007.

Chapter 7

1. There are many such studies, usually of a single program. A recent example is Algozzine, Gretes, Queen, & Cowan-Hathcock, 2007.

2. Hansford, Tennent, & Ehrich, 2003.

3. Long, 1997.

4. Graham, 1997.

5. Ehrich, Hansford, & Tennent, 2004.

6. Hansford et al., 2003, p. 2.

7. Tellez, 1992.

8. This is something we have witnessed at the New Teacher Center with new teachers responding to our online induction survey. Over the past 10 years we have surveyed upwards of 100,000 teachers most of whom express great satisfaction with the formal mentoring they receive, but state also that they value to an even higher degree the support they receive from their teaching colleagues. This finding does not go counter to the intentions of the NTC model, where mentors encourage the beginning teachers to develop collaborative relations and networks with their fellow teachers.

References

Aaronson, D., Barrow, L., & Sander, W. (2007). Teachers and student achievement in the Chicago public high schools. *Journal of Labor Economics, 25*(1), 95–135.

Achinstein, B., & Barrett, A. (2004). (Re)Framing classroom contexts: How new teachers and mentors view diverse learners and challenges of practice. *Teachers College Record, 106*(4), 716–746.

Algozzine, B., Gretes, J., Queen, A. J., & Cowan-Hathcock, M. (2007). Beginning teachers' perceptions of their induction program experiences. *Clearing House: A Journal of Educational Strategies, Issues, and Ideas, 80*(3), 137–143.

Allen, T. D., Eby, L. T., Poteet, M. L., Lentz, E., & Lima, L. (2004). Career benefits associated with mentoring for protégés: A meta-analysis. *Journal of Applied Psychology, 89*(1), 127–136.

Amidon, E. J., & Hough, J. (1967). *Interaction analysis: Theory, research, and application.* Reading, MA: Addison-Wesley.

Amrein-Beardsley, A. (2008). Methodological concerns about the education value-added assessment system. *Educational Researcher, 37*(2), 65–75.

Arnold, C. (1992). An introduction to hierarchical linear models. *Measurement and Evaluation in Counseling and Development, 25*(2), 58–90.

Ashburn, E. (1987). Current developments in teacher induction programs. *Action in Teacher Education, 8*(4), 4–44.

Association of Community Organizations for Reform Now (ACORN) (2003, June). *Where have all the teachers gone? The costs of teacher turnover in ACORN neighborhood schools in Chicago.* Retrieved February 2, 2008, from http://www.acorn.org/index.php?id=315

Association of Teacher Educators. (1989). *Assisting the beginning teacher.* Reston, VA: Author.

Athanases, S. Z., & Achinstein, B. (2003). Focusing new teachers on individual and low-performing students: The centrality of formative assessment in the mentor's repertoire of practice. *Teachers College Record, 105*(8), 1486–1520.

Bacharach, S. B., Bamberger, P., Conley, S. C., & Bauer, S. (1990). The dimensionality of decision participation in educational organizations: The value of a multi-domain evaluative approach. *Educational Administration Quarterly, 26*(2), 126–167.

Bacon, F. (1902). *Novum organum*. Edited by Joseph Devey. New York: P. F. Collier. (Original work published in 1621)

Ballou, D. (1996). Do public schools hire the best applicants? *Quarterly Journal of Economics, 111*(1), 97–133.

Ballou, D. (2002). Sizing up test scores. *Education Next, 2*(2), 10–15.

Ballou, D., & Podgursky, M. (1998). Teacher recruitment and retention in public and private schools. *Journal of Policy Analysis and Management, 17*(3), 393–417.

Ballou, D., Sanders, W., & Wright, P. (2004). Controlling for student background in value-added assessment of teachers. *Journal of Educational and Behavioral Statistics, 29*(1), 37–65.

Barnes, G., Crowe, E., & Schaefer, B. (2007). *The cost of teacher turnover in five school districts: A pilot study*. Washington, DC: National Commission on Teaching and America's Future (NCTAF). Retrieved February 2, 2008, from: http://www.nctaf.org/resources/demonstration_projects/turnover/documents/CTTFullReportfinal.pdf.

Barnett, W. S. (1985). Benefit-cost analysis of the Perry Preschool Program and its policy implications. *Educational Evaluation and Policy Analysis, 7*(4), 333–342.

Becklen R., & Cervone D. (1983). Selective looking and the noticing of unexpected events. *Memory and Cognition, 11*(6), 601–608.

Belfield, C. R. (2003, April). Estimating the rate of return to educational investments: A case study using the Big Brothers Big Sisters mentoring program. New York: National Center for the Study of Privatization in Education, Teachers College, Columbia University. Retrieved on February 24, 2008 from http://www.ncspe.org/publications_files/bbbs.pdf.

Berliner, D. (1986). In pursuit of the expert pedagogue. *Educational Researcher, 15*(1), 5–13.

Billingsley, B. S. (1993). Teacher retention and attrition in special and general education: A critical review of the literature. *Journal of Special Education, 27*(2), 137–174.

Billingsley, B. S. (2004). Special education teacher retention and attrition: A critical analysis of the research literature. *Journal of Special Education, 38*(1), 39–55.

Billingsley, B. S., & Cross, L. H. (1992). Predictors of commitment, job satisfaction, and intent to stay in teaching. A comparison of general and special educators. *Journal of Special Education, 23*(4), 453–471.

Blair-Larsen, S. (1998). Designing a mentoring program. *Education, 18*(4), 602–604.

Bobbitt, S. A., Faupel, E., & Burns, S. (1991). *Characteristics of stayers, movers, and leavers: Results from the teacher follow up survey, 1988–89*. Washington, DC: National Center for Education Statistics.

Bobbitt, S. A., Leich, M. C., Whitener, S. D., & Lynch, H. R. (1994). *Characteristics of stayers, movers, and leavers: Results from the teacher follow-up survey: 1991–92*. Washington, DC: National Center for Education Statistics.

Boe, E. E., Bobbitt, S. A., & Cook, L. H. (1997). Whither didst thou go? Retention, reassignment, migration, and attrition of special and general education teachers from a national perspective *The Journal of Special Education, 30*(Winter), 371–389.

Boe, E. E., Cook, L. H., Kaufman, M. J., & Danielson, L. (1995). *Special and general education teachers in public schools: Sources of supply in national perspective.* (Research Report 1995-TSD1). Philadelphia: University of Pennsylvania, Graduate School of Education, Center for Research and Evaluation in Social Policy.

Bowers, G. R., & Eberhart, N. A. (1988). Mentors and the entry- year program. *Theory Into Practice, 27*(3), 226–236.

Braun, H. (1988). A new approach to avoiding problems of scale in interpreting trends in mental measurement data. *Journal of Educational Measurement, 25*(3), 171–191.

Britton, T., & Paine, L. (2005). Applying ideas from other countries. In H. Portner (Ed.), *Teacher mentoring and induction* (pp. 213–223). Thousand Oaks, CA: Corwin Press.

Britton, E., Paine, L., Pimm, D., & Raizen, S. (Eds.). (2003). *Comprehensive teacher induction: Systems for early career learning.* Dordrecht, Netherlands: Kluwer Academic Publishers & WestEd.

Brophy, J., & Good, T. L. (1986). Teacher behavior and student achievement. In M. C. Wittrock (Ed.), *Handbook of research on teaching* (3rd ed., pp. 328–375). New York: Macmillan.

Broughman, S., & Rollefson, M. (2000). Teacher supply in the United States: Sources of newly hired teachers in public and private schools: 1987–88 to 1993–94. *Education Statistics Quarterly, 2*(3), 28–32.

Brown, J. G., & Wambach, C. (1987). *Using mentors to increase new teacher retention: The mentor teacher induction project.* Paper presented at the annual meeting of the American Association of Colleges for Teacher Education, Arlington, VA. (ERIC Document Reproduction Service No. ED 280816)

Bruner, J. S. & Postman, L. (1949). On the perception of incongruity: A paradigm. *Journal of Personality, 18*(2), 206–223.

Bruner, J. S. & Potter, M. C. (1964). Interference in visual recognition. *Science, 144*(3617), 424–425.

Cain, G. G. & Watts, H. W. (1970). Problems in Making Policy Inferences from the Coleman Report. *American Sociological Review, 35*(2), 228–242.

California Commission on Teacher Credentialing (CCTC) & California Department of Education (CDE). (1997). *California standards for the teaching profession.* Retrieved December 3, 2007, from http://www.ctc.ca.gov/reports/cstpreport.pdf.

California Commission on Teacher Credentialing (CCTC) (2002). *Preliminary report on teacher retention in California.* Retrieved August 1, 2004, from http://134.186.81.70/reports/PrelimRptOnTeacherRetInCA.pdf.

California Council on Teacher Education (CCTE) (2002). *Standards of quality and effectiveness for teacher induction programs.* Retrieved August 1, 2004, from http://ccbtsa.org/pdfs/ProgStndrds.pdf.

Chaiken, S., & Trope, Y. (Eds.). (1999). *Dual-process theories in social psychology.* New York: Guilford Press.

Chapman, D. W. (1984). Teacher retention: The test of a model. *American Educational Research Journal, 21*(3), 645–658.

Chapman, D. W. & Green, M.S. (1986). Teacher retention: A further examination. *Journal of Educational Research, 79*(5),273–279.

Charles A. Dana Center. (2002). *Texas beginning educator support system: Evaluation report for year three, 2001–02.* Austin: University of Texas. Retrieved August 1, 2004, from http://www.sbec.state.tx.us/SBECOnline/txbess/evalrpt.asp.

Cheng, M., & Brown, R. S. (1992). *A two-year evaluation of the peer support pilot project: 1990–1992.* Toronto, Ontario, Canada: Toronto Board of Education, Research Department. (ERIC Document Reproduction Service No. ED 356 204).

Christensen-Szalanski, J. J. (1991). The hindsight bias: A meta- analysis. *Organizational Behavior and Human Decision Processes, 48*(1), 147–168.

Clark, C. M., & Peterson, P. L. (1986). Teachers' thought processes. In M. C. Wittrock (Ed.), *Handbook of research on teaching* (3rd ed., pp. 255–296). New York: Macmillan.

Clotfelter, C. T., Ladd, H. F., & Vigdor, J. L. (2006). *Teacher-student matching and the assessment of teacher effectiveness* (NBER Working Paper No. W11936). Cambridge, MA: National Bureau of Economic Research. Retrieved February 4, 2008, from http://papers.ssrn.com/sol3/papers.cfm?abstract_id=883069.

Cochran-Smith, M. (2004). Defining the outcomes of teacher education: What's social justice got to do with it? *Asia-Pacific Journal of Teacher Education, 32*(3), 193–212.

Cochran-Smith, M., & Fries, M. K. (2001). Sticks, stones and ideology: The discourse of reform in teacher education. *Educational Researcher, 30*(8), 3–15.

Coleman, J. S., Campbell, E., Hobson, C., McPartland, J., Mood, A., Weinfeld, R., & York, R. (1966). *Equality of educational opportunity.* Washington, DC: Government Printing Office.

Connecticut State Department of Education. (2007-2008). *A guide to the BEST program for beginning teachers, 2007–2008.* Retrieved January 1, 2008, from http://www.sde.ct.gov/sde/lib/sde/PDF/BEST/begininngteaching-guide/bt_guide.pdf.

Connolly, R. A. (2000). Why do good teachers leave the profession? What can be done to retain them? *Momentum, 31*(3), 55–57.

Corcoran, S. P., Evans, W. N., & Schwab, R. M. (2004). Changing labor-market opportunities for women and the quality of teachers, 1957–2000. *The American Economic Review, 94*(2), 230–235.

Costa, A., & Garmston, R. (1994). *Cognitive coaching: A foundation for renaissance schools.* Norwood, MA: Christopher-Gordon.

Cox, D.R. (1972), Regression models and life tables. *Journal of the Royal Statistical Society, B 34,* 187–220.

Cox, T., & Griffiths, A. (1995). *Occupational stress and burn-out of teachers: A review* (Sectoral Activities Programme Working Paper, SAP 4.32/WP.84). Geneva: ILO/UNESCO.

Daneshvary, N., & Clauretie, T. (2001). Efficiency and costs in education: Year-round versus traditional schedules. *Economics of Education Review, 20*(3), 279–287.

Danielson, C. (2007). *Enhancing professional practice: A framework for teaching.* Alexandria, VA: Association for Supervision and Curriculum Development.

Danielson, C., & McGreal, T. L. (2000). *Teacher evaluation to enhance professional practice.* Alexandria, VA: Association for Supervision and Curriculum Development.

Darling-Hammond, L. (2000). *Solving the dilemmas of teacher supply, demand, and standards: How we can ensure a competent, caring, and qualified teacher for every child.* New York: National Commission on Teaching and America's Future.

Darling-Hammond, L. (2001). The challenge of staffing our schools. *Educational Leadership, 58*(8), 12–17.

Darling-Hammond, L. (2002, October 1). Access to quality teaching: an analysis of inequality in California's public schools. Williams Watch Series: Investigating the Claims of Williams v. State of California. Los Angeles: UCLA's Institute for Democracy, Education, & Access. Retrieved January 12, 2008, from http://repositories.cdlib.org/idea/wws/wws-rr002-1002.

Darling-Hammond, L., & Wise, A. E. (1983). Teaching standards, or standardized teaching? *Educational Leadership, 41*(2), 66–69.

Davis, F. D., Lohse, G. L., & Kottemann, J. E. (1994). Harmful effects of seemingly helpful information on forecasts of stock earnings. *Journal of Economic Psychology, 15*(2), 253–267.

Delandshere, G. (1994). The assessment of teachers in the United States. *Assessment in Education, 1*(1), 95–113.

Dolton, P., & Van der Klaauw, W. (1995). Leaving teaching in the UK: A duration analysis. *Economic Journal, 105*(429), 431–444.

Dolton, P., & Van der Klaauw, W. (1999). The turnover of teachers: A competing risks explanation. *Review of Economics and Statistics, 81*(3), 543–552.

Duncan, M. J., & Biddle, B. J. (1974). *The study of teaching.* New York: Holt, Rinehart, & Winston.

Dupre, B. B. (1986). Problems regarding the survival of future Black teachers in education. *Journal of Negro Education, 55*(1), 56–66.

Earley, P., & Ross, S. (2006). Teacher recruitment and retention: Policy history and new challenges. In *Teacher recruitment and retention: How do we get and keep teachers?* Amherst, MA: National Evaluation Systems.

Eberhard, J., Reinhardt-Mondragon, P., & Stottlemyer, B. (2000). *Strategies for new teacher retention: Creating a climate of authentic professional development for teachers with three or less years of experience.* Corpus Christi, TX: South Texas Research and Development Center, Texas A&M University. Retrieved September 16, 2008, from http://www.eric.ed.gov. (ERIC Document Reproduction Service No. ED450116).

Edwards K., & Smith E. E. (1996). A disconfirmation bias in the evaluation of arguments. *Journal of Personality and Social Psychology, 71*(1), 5–24.

Ehrenberg, R., & Brewer, D. (1994). Do school and teacher characteristics matter? Evidence from high school and beyond. *Economics of Education Review, 13*(1), 1–17.

Ehrenberg, R., & Brewer, D. (1995). Did teachers' verbal ability and race matter in the 1960s? *Coleman* revisited. *Economics of Education Review, 14*(1), 1–21.

Ehrich, L. C., Hansford, B., & Tennent, L. (2004). Formal mentoring programs in education and other professions: A review of the literature. *Educational Administration Quarterly, 40*(4), 518–540.

Eisenschmidt, E. (2006). *Implementation of induction year for novice teachers in Estonia.* Dissertation on Social Sciences. Tallinn University, Tallinn, Estonia. Retrieved on January 5, 2008 from http://www.tlulib.ee/files/arts/24/sots23b56ef6e91f94339f43b5abaecd0ee3d.pdf.

Elmore, C. J. (2003). Using full-time mentor teacher consultants and part-time peer mentors in Wicomico County, Maryland, public schools: The impact on new teacher effectiveness and retention. *Dissertation Abstracts International, 63*(12), 4277.

Ensher, E. A., & Murphy, S. E. (1997). Effects of race, gender, perceived similarity, and contact on mentor relationships. *Journal of Vocational Behavior, 50*(3), 460–481.

Epstein, S. (1994). Integration of the cognitive and psychodynamic unconscious. *American Psychologist, 49*(8), 709–724.

Evertson, C. M., & Smithey, M. W. (2000). Mentoring effects on protégés' classroom practice: An experimental field study. *Journal of Educational Research, 93*(5), 294–304.

Falch, T., & Strøm, B. (2003). *Teacher turnover and non-pecuniary factors.* Working Paper Series No. 1/2004. Trondheim, Norway: Norwegian University of Science and Technology. Retrieved July 20, 2004, from http://www.svt.ntnu.no/iso/wp/wp.htm

Farkas, S., Johnson, J., & Foleno, T. (2000). *A sense of calling: Who teaches and why.* New York: Public Agenda.

Feiman-Nemser, S. (2001). Helping novices learn to teach: Lessons from an exemplary support teacher. *Journal of Teacher Education, 52*(1), 17–30.

Feiman-Nemser, S., Carver, C., Schwille, S., & Yusko, B. (1999). Beyond support: Taking new teachers seriously as learners. In M. Scherer (Ed.), *A better beginning: Supporting and mentoring new teachers* (pp. 8–12). Alexandria, VA: Association for Supervision and Curriculum Development.

Feiman-Nemser, S., & Parker, M. (1992). *Mentoring in Context: A Comparison of Two U.S. Programs for Beginning Teachers.* (NCRTL Special Report). Retrieved January 20, 2008, from http://ncrtl.msu.edu/http/sreports/spring92.pdf.

Fenstermacher, G. D., & Richardson, V. (2005). On making determinations of quality in teaching. *Teachers College Record, 107*(1), 186–213.

Ferguson, R. (1991). Paying for public education: New evidence on how and why money matters? *Harvard Journal on Legislation, 28*(2), 465–498.

Ferguson, R. F. & Ladd, H. F. (1996). How and why money matters: An analysis of Alabama schools. In H. F. Ladd (Ed.), *Holding schools accountable:*

Performance-based reform in education (pp. 265–268). Washington, DC: Brookings Institution.

Fideler, E., & Haselkorn, D. (1999). *Learning the ropes: Urban teacher induction practices in the United States.* Belmont, MA: Recruiting New Teachers.

Fischer, G. A. (1967). Measuring ambiguity. *The American Journal of Psychology, 80*(4), 541–557.

Fischhoff, B. (2001). Learning from experience: Coping with hindsight bias and ambiguity. In J. S. Armstrong (Ed.), *Principles of Forecasting* (pp. 484–494). Norwell, MA: Kluwer Academic Press.

Fischhoff, B., & Beyth, R. (1975). "I knew it would happen": Remembered probabilities of once-future things. *Organizational Behavior and Human Performance, 13*(1), 1–16.

Flanders, N. A. (1970). *Analyzing teacher behavior.* Reading, MA: Addison-Wesley.

Fletcher, S. H., Strong, M., & Villar, A. (2008). An investigation of the effects of variations in mentor-based induction on the performance of students in California. *Teachers College Record, 110*(10). Retrieved April 7, 2008, from http://www.tcrecord.org/library/Abstract.asp?ContentID=14719

Flyer, F., & Rosen, S. (1997). The new economics of teachers and education. *Journal of Labor Economics, 15*(1), S104–139.

Fraser, J. (2003). *Investing today for tomorrow: The costs and benefits of early childhood care and education* (Special Report). Pittsburgh, PA: University of Pittsburgh Office of Child Development. Retrieved April 20, 2008 from http://www.education.pitt.edu/ocd/publications/sr2003-06.pdf

Frederick, S. (2005). Cognitive reflection and decision making. *Journal of Economic Perspectives, 19*(4), 25–42.

Fuerst, J. S. & Fuerst, D. (1993). Chicago experience with an early childhood program: The special case of the Child Parent Center Program. *Urban Education, 28*(1), 69–96.

Fuller, E. (2003). *Beginning teacher retention rates for TxBESS and non-TxBESS teachers* (Report). Austin, TX: State Board for Educator Certification.

Furtwengler, C. B. (1995). Beginning teachers programs: Analysis of state actions during the reform era. *Education Policy Analysis Archives, 3*(3).Retrieved April 1, 2008, from http://epaa.asu.ed/epaa/v3n3.html

Gallagher, H. A. (2004). Vaughn Elementary's innovative teacher evaluation system: Are teacher evaluation scores related to growth in student achievement? *Peabody Journal of Education, 79*(4), 79–107.

Ganser, T. (2002). The new teacher mentors: Four trends that are changing the look of mentoring programs for new teachers. *American School Board Journal, 189*(12), 25–27.

Ganser, T. (2005). Learning from the past—Building for the future. In H. Portner (Ed.), *Teacher Mentoring and Induction: The State of the Art and Beyond* (pp. 3–20). Thousand Oaks, CA: Corwin Press.

Gehrke, N. J. (1988). Toward a definition of mentoring. *Theory Into Practice, 27*(3), 190–194.

Gehrke, N. J., & Kay, R. S. (1984). The socialization of beginning teachers through mentor-protégé relationships. *Journal of Teacher Education,* 35(3), 21–24.

Gersten, R., Keating, T., Yobanoff, P., & Harniss, M. K. (2001). Working in special education: Factors that enhance special educators' intent to stay. *Exceptional Children, 67*(4), 549–567.

Gitomer, D., Latham, A., & Ziomek, R. (1999). *The academic quality of prospective teachers: The impact of admissions and licensure testing.* Princeton, NJ: Educational Testing Service.

Gladwell, M. (2005). *Blink: The power of thinking without thinking.* New York: Little Brown.

Glazerman, S., Dolfin, S., Bleeker, M., Johnson, A., Isenberg, E., Lugo-Gil, J., Grider, M., & Britton, E. (2008). *Impacts of comprehensive teacher induction: Results from the first year of a randomized controled study.* Available online at http://www.mathematica-mpr.com/publications/redirect_pubsdb.asp?strSite=pdfs/teachinduction1.pdf.

Glazerman, S., Senesky, S., Seftor, N., & Johnson, A. (2006). *Design of an impact evaluation of teacher induction programs* (Final Report No. 6137–070). Washington, DC: Mathematica Policy Research, Inc. Retrieved February 5, 2008, from http://www.mathematica-mpr.com/publications/PDFs/designimpact.pdf.

Gold, M. (1987). *Retired teachers as consultants to new teachers: A new inservice teacher training model* (Final Report). Washington, DC: American Association of State Colleges and Universities.

Goldhaber, D. (2002). The mystery of good teaching: Surveying the evidence on student achievement and teachers' characteristics. *Education Next 2*(1), 50–55.

Goldhaber, D., & Anthony, E. (2007). Can teacher quality be effectively assessed? National Board Certification as a signal of effective teaching. *Review of Economics and Statistics, 89*(1), 134–150.

Goldhaber, D., & Brewer, D. J. (2000). Does teacher certification matter? High school teacher certification status and student achievement. *Educational Evaluation and Policy Analysis, 22*(2), 129–145.

Goldhaber, D., Brewer, D. J., & Anderson, D. (1999). A three-way error components analysis of educational productivity. *Education Economics, 7*(3), 199–208.

Goldhaber, D., Gross, B., & Player, D. (2007, October). *Are public schools really losing their "best"? Assessing the career transitions of teachers and their implications for the quality of the teacher workforce* (Working Paper No. 12). Washington, DC: CALDER, Urban Institute. Retrieved April 5, 2008, from http://www.caldercenter.org/PDF/1001115_Public_Schools.pdf.

Goldstein, J. (2004). Making sense of distributed leadership: The case of Peer Assistance and Review. *Educational Evaluation and Policy Analysis, 26*(2), 173–197. (Reprinted with apology; published originally in *Educational Evaluation and Policy Analysis 25*(4), 397–421)

Goldstein, J. (2007). Easy to dance to: Solving the problems of teacher evaluation with peer assistance and review. *American Journal of Education, 113*(3), 479–508. Available online at http://www.journals.uchicago.edu/loi/aje/.

Gordon, J. (1994). Why students of color are not entering teaching: Reflections from minority teachers. *Journal of Teacher Education, 45*(5), 346–353.

Graham, P. (1997). Tensions in the mentor teacher-student teacher relationship: Creating productive sites for learning within a high school English teacher education program. *Teaching and Teacher Education, 13*(5), 513–527.

Gramlich, E. M. (1998). *A guide to benefit-cost analysis* (2nd ed.). Prospect Heights, IL: Waveland Press.

Grant, L. L. (2004). Meta-analysis of induction and mentoring programs' contribution to new teacher retention during the first five years of employment. *Dissertation Abstracts International, 64*(12), 4287.

Gregory, R. L. (1980). Perceptions as hypotheses. *Philosophical Transactions of the Royal Society of London. Series B, Biological Sciences: Vol. 290, No. 1038, The Psychology of Vision* (pp. 181–197).

Gregory, R. L. (1997). Knowledge in perception and illusion. *Philosophical Transactions of the Royal Society of London: Series B, Biological Sources, Vol. 352, No. 1358. Knowledge-based vision in man and machine* (pp. 1121–1128).

Green, J. E., & Weaver, R. A. (1992). Who aspires to teach? A descriptive study of preservice teachers. *Contemporary Education, 63*(3), 234–238.

Grissmer, D. W., & Kirby, S. (1992). *Patterns of attrition among Indiana teachers.* Santa Monica, CA: RAND.

Grissmer, D. W., & Kirby, S. N. (1997). Teacher turnover and teacher quality. *Teachers College Record, 99*(1), 45–56.

Gritz, R., & Theobald, N. (1996). The effects of school district spending priorities on length of stay in teaching. *Journal of Human Resources, 31*(3), 477–512.

Grossman, J. B., & Tierney, J. P. (1998). Does mentoring work? An impact study of the Big Brothers Big Sisters program. *Evaluation Review, 22*(3), 403–426.

Guarino, C., Santibañez, L., & Daley, G. (2006). Teacher recruitment and retention: A review of the recent empirical literature. *Review of Educational Research, 76*(2), 173–208.

Haberman, M. (1999). Increasing the number of high-quality African American teachers in urban schools. *Journal of Instructional Psychology, 26*(4), 208–212.

Haberman, M. (2001). The creation of an urban normal school: What constitutes quality in alternative certification? *Educational Studies, 32*(3), 278–288.

Hall, J. L., Johnson, B., & Bowman, A. C. (1995). Teacher socialization: A spiral process. *Teacher Educator, 30*(4), 25–36.

Hansford, B., Tennent, L. & Ehrich, L. C. (2003). Educational mentoring: Is it worth the effort? *Education, Research and Perspectives, 30*(1), 42–75.

Hanushek, E. A. (1986). The economics of schooling: production and efficiency in public schools. *Journal of Economic Literature, 24*(3), 1141–1178.

Hanushek, E. A. (1992). The trade-off between child quantity and quality. *Journal of Political Economy, 100*(1), 84–117.

Hanushek, E. A. (1997). Assessing the effects of school resources on student performance: An update. *Educational Evaluation and Policy Analysis 19*(2), 141–164.

Hanushek, E. A. (2001). Black–White achievement differences and governmental interventions. *American Economic Review 91*(2), 24–28.

Hanushek, E. A., & Kain, J. F. (1972). On the value of "equality of educational opportunity" as a guide to public policy. In F. Mosteller & D. P. Moynihan (Eds.), *On equality of educational opportunity* (pp. 116–145). New York: Random House.

Hanushek, E.A., Kain, J.F., O'Brien, D.M., & Rivkin, S.G. (2005). *The market for teacher quality.* (NBER Working Paper 11154). Cambridge, MA: National Bureau of Economic Research.

Hanushek, E. A., Kain, J. F., & Rivkin, S. G. (1999). *Do higher salaries buy better teachers?* National Bureau of Economic Research working paper no. 7082.

Hanushek, E. A., Kain, J. F., & Rivkin, S. G. (2001, November). *Why public schools lose teachers.* (NBER Working Paper No. 8599). Retrieved July 2, 2004, from http://www.nber.org/papers/w8599.

Hanushek, E. A., Kain, J. F., & Rivkin, S. G. (2004). Why public schools lose teachers. *Journal of Human Resources, 39*(2), 326–354.

Hanushek, E. A. & Pace, R. R. (1995). Who chooses to teach (and why)? *Economics of Education Review, 14*(2), 101–117.

Hargreaves, A., & Fullan, M. (2000). Mentoring in the new millennium. *Theory Into Practice, 39*(1), 50–56.

Harmon, H. (2001, March 1–4). *Attracting and retaining teachers in rural areas.* Paper presented at the annual meeting of the American Association of College Teachers of Education, Dallas, TX.

Harris, D. N. & Adams, S. J. (2007). Understanding the level and causes of teacher turnover: A comparison with other professions. *Economics of Education Review, 26*(3), 325–337.

Harris, D. N. & Sass, T. R. (2007). *Teacher training, teacher quality, and student achievement* (Working Paper No. 3). Washington, DC: CALDER, Urban Institute.

Hawkins, S. A., & Hastie, R. (1990). Hindsight: Biased judgments of past events after the outcomes are known. *Psychological Bulletin, 107*(3), 311–327.

Heaton, C., & Throsby, D. (1998). Benefit-cost analysis of foreign student flows from developing countries: The case of postgraduate education. *Economics of Education Review, 17*(2), 117–126.

Henke, R., Chen, X., Geis, S., & Knepper, P. (2000). *Progress through the teacher pipeline: 1992–93 college graduates and elementary/secondary teaching as of 1997.* Washington, DC: National Center for Education Statistics.

Henke, R. R., & Zahn, L. (2001). Attrition of new teachers among recent college graduates. Washington, DC: National Center for Education Statistics.

Henry, M. A. (1988). Multiple support: A successful model for inducting first-year teachers. *Teacher Educator, 24*(2), 7–12.

Herrnstein, R. J. (1997). *The matching law.* Beverly Hills, CA: Russell Sage Foundation.

Heyns, B. (1988). Educational defectors: A first look at teacher attrition in the NLS-72. *Educational Researcher, 17*, 24–32.

Hoff, D. J. (2007, February 13). NCLB panel calls for federal role in setting national standards. *Education Week, 26.* Retrieved April 5, 2008, from http://www.edweek.org/ew/articles/2007/02/13/23aspen_web.h26.html.

Hood, S., & Parker, L. J. (1994). Minority students informing the faculty: Implications for racial diversity and the future of teacher education. *Journal of Teacher Education, 45*(3), 164–171.

Hughes, B. E. (1970). *Evaluation report of the bilingual education program: Harlandale Independent School District, Sun Marcos Independent School District, 1969–70.* Harlandale: Southwest Texas State University. (ERIC Document Reproduction Service No. 055-686).

Huling-Austin, L. (1989). Beginning teacher assistance programs: An overview. In *Assisting the beginning teacher* (pp. 5–13). Reston, VA: Association of Teacher Educators.

Hummel-Rossi, B., & Ashdown, J. (2002). The state of cost-benefit and cost-effectiveness analyses in education. *Review of Education Research, 72*(1), 1–30.

Hunt, D. M., & Michael, C. (1983). Mentorship: A career training and development tool. *Academy of Management Review, 8*(3), 475–485.

Imazeki, J. (2002). Teacher Attrition and Mobility in Urban Districts: Evidence from Wisconsin. In C. Roelke & J. K. Rice (Eds.), *Fiscal issues in urban schools* (pp. 119–136). Greenwich, CT: Information Age Publishing Inc.

Ingersoll, R. M. (1997). *Teacher professionalization and teacher commitment: A multilevel analysis.* Washington, DC: National Center for Education Statistics.

Ingersoll, R. M. (2000). A different approach to solving the teacher shortage problem. *Policy Perspectives, 2*(2), 1–6.

Ingersoll, R. M. (2001). Teacher turnover and teacher shortages: An organizational analysis. *American Education Research Journal, 38*(3), 499–534.

Ingersoll, R. M. (2002). The teacher shortage: A case of wrong diagnosis and wrong prescription. *NASSP Bulletin, 86*(631), 16–31.

Ingersoll, R. M. (2003). *Is there really a teacher shortage?* Seattle: University of Washington, Center for the Study of Teaching and Policy. Retrieved June 6, 2007, from: http://www.gse.upenn.edu/inpress/Is%20There%20Really%20a%20Teacher%20Shortage.pdf.

Ingersoll, R. M. (2007). Teacher turnover and teacher quality: the recurring myth of teacher shortages. *Teachers College Record, 99*(1), 41–44.

Ingersoll, R. M., Alsalam, N., Quinn, P. & Bobbit, S. (1997). *Teacher professionalization and teacher commitment: A multilevel analysis* (NCES No. 97-069). Washington, DC: National Center for Educational Statistics.

Ingersoll, R. M., & Kralik, J.M. (2004). *The impact of mentoring on teacher retention: What the research says.* ECS Research Review, Denver, CO: Educational Commission of the States. Retrieved June 30, 2004, from http://www.ecs.org/clearinghouse/50/36/5036.pdf.

Ingersoll, R. M., & Smith, T. (2003). The wrong solution to the teacher shortage. *Educational Leadership, 60*(8), 30–33.

Jacob, B., & Lefgren, L. (2008). Can principals identify effective teachers? Evidence on subjective performance evaluation in education. *Journal of Labor*

Economics, 26(1), 101–136.

James, W. (1950). *The principles of psychology.* New York: Dover. (Originally published 1890)

Jennings, E. E. (1971). *Routes to the executive suite.* New York: McGraw-Hill.

Johnson, S. M., & The Project on the Next Generation of Teachers. (2004). *Finders and keepers: Helping teachers survive and thrive in our schools.* San Francisco: Jossey-Bass.

Johnson-Laird, P. N. (1983). *Mental models.* Cambridge, MA: Harvard University Press.

Jones, D. L., & Sandidge, R. F. (1997). Recruiting and retaining teachers in urban schools: implications for policy and the law. *Education and Urban Society, 29*(2), 192–203.

Kagan, D. (1992). Professional growth among preservice and beginning teachers. *Review of Educational Research, 62*(2), 129–169.

Kahneman, D. (2002, December 8). *Maps of bounded rationality: A perspective on intuitive judgment and choice* (Nobel Prize Lecture). Retrieved on February 29, 2008 from http://nobelprize.org/nobel_prizes/economics/laureates/2002/kahnemann-lecture.pdf.

Kahneman, D., & Frederick, S. (2002, December 8). Representativeness revisited: Attribute substitution in intuitive judgment. In T. Gilovich, D. Griffin, & D. Kahneman (Eds.), *Heuristics and biases* (pp. 49–81). New York: Cambridge University Press.

Kahneman, D., & Frederick, S. (2005). A model of heuristic judgment. In K. J. Holyoak & R. G. Morrison (Eds.), *The Cambridge handbook of thinking and reasoning* (pp. 267–293). Cambridge: Cambridge University Press.

Kane, T. J., Rockoff, J. E., & Staiger, D. O. (2006). *What does certification tell us about teacher effectiveness? Evidence from New York City* (Working Paper No. 12155). Cambridge, MA: National Bureau Of Economic Research. Retrieved January 12, 2008, from: http://www.nber.org/papers/w12155.

Kane, T. J., & Staiger, D. O. (2002). The promise and pitfalls of using imprecise school accountability measures. *The Journal of Economic Perspectives, 16*(4), 91–114.

Kapadia, K., Coca, V., & Easton, J. Q. (2007). *Keeping new teachers: A first look at the influences of induction in the Chicago Public Schools.* Chicago: Consortium on Chicago School Research, University of Chicago.

Kelley, L. (2004). Why induction matters. *Journal of Teacher Education, 55*(5), 438–448.

Kelman, S. (1981, January/February). Cost-benefit analysis: An ethical critique. *AEI Journal on Government and Society Regulations,* pp. 33–40.

Kimball, S. M., White, B., Milanowski, A. T., & Borman, G. (2004). Examining the relationship between teacher evaluation and student assessment results in Washoe County. *Peabody Journal of Education, 79*(4), 54–78.

Kirby, S., Berends, M., & Naftel, S. (1999). Supply and demand of minority teachers in Texas: Problems and prospects. *Educational Evaluation and Policy Analysis, 21*(1), 47–66.

Kirby, S. N., & Grissmer, D.W. (1993). *Teacher attrition: Theory, evidence, and suggested policy options.* Santa Monica, CA: Rand.

Kirby, S. N., Grissmer, D. W., & Hudson, L. (1991). Sources of teacher supply: Some new evidence from Indiana. *Educational Evaluation and Policy Analysis, 13*(3), 256–268.

Klug, B. J., & Salzman, S. A. (1991). Formal induction vs. informal mentoring: Comparative effects and outcomes. *Teaching and Teacher Education, 7*(3), 241–251.

Kram, K. E. (1985). *Mentoring at work: Developmental relationships in organizational life.* Glenview, IL: Scott, Foresman & Co.

Kunda, Z. (1990). The case for motivated reasoning. *Psychological Bulletin, 108*(3), 480–498.

Kupermintz, H. (2003). Teacher effects and teacher effectiveness: A validity investigation of the Tennessee Value Added Assessment System. *Educational Evaluation and Policy Analysis, 25*(3), 287–298.

Kyriacou, C. (1989). Teacher stress and burnout: An international review. *Educational Research, 29*(2), 146–152.

Kyriacou, C. (2001). Teacher stress: Directions for future research. *Educational Review, 53*(1), 27–35.

Laczko-Kerr, I., & Berliner, D. C. (2002). The effectiveness of "Teach for America" and other under-certified teachers on student academic achievement: A case of harmful public policy." *Education Policy Analysis Archives, 10*(37). Retrieved January 25, 2007, from http://epaa.asu.edu/epaa/v10n37/

Lambur, M., Rajgopal, R., Lewis, E., Cox, R., & Ellerbrock, M. (2003). Applying cost benefit analysis to nutrition education programs: Focus on the Virginia Expanded Food and Nutrition Program (Publication No. 490–403). Blacksburg: Virginia Polytechnic Institute and State University, Virgina Cooperative Extension. Retrieved April 19, 2008, from: http://www.ext.vt.edu/pubs/nutrition/490-403/490-403.html.

Lankford, M., Loeb, S., & Wyckoff, J. (2002). Teacher sorting and the plight of urban schools: A descriptive analysis. *Educational Evaluation and Policy Analysis, 24*(1), 37–62.

LaShier, W. S. (1967). The use of interaction analysis in BSCS laboratory block classrooms. *Journal of Teacher Education, 18*(4), 439–446.

Latham, N. I. & Vogt, P. W. (2007). Do Professional Development Schools Reduce Teacher Attrition?: Evidence from a Longitudinal Study of 1,000 graduates. *Journal of Teacher Education, 58*(2), 153–167.

Lavely, C., Berger, N., Blackman, J., Follman, J., & McCarthy, J. (1994). Contemporary teacher classroom performance observation instruments. *Education, 114*(4), 618–625.

Lazovsky, R., & Reichenberg, R. (2006). The new mandatory induction programme for all beginning teachers in Israel: perceptions of inductees in five study tracks. *Journal of Education for Teaching, 32*(1), 53–70.

Littleton, M., Tally-Foos, K., & Wolaver, R. (1992). Mentoring: A support system for new teachers. *Clearing House, 65*(3), 172–174.

Liu, X. S. (2007). The effect of teacher influence at school on first-year teacher attrition: A multilevel analysis of the Schools and Staffing Survey for

1999–2000. *Educational Research and Evaluation, 13*(1), 1–16.

Long, J. (1997). The dark side of mentoring. *Australian Educational Research, 24*(2), 115–123.

Lucksinger, L. N. (2000). Teachers: Can we get them and keep them? *The Delta Kappa Gamma Bulletin, 67*(1) 11–15.

Luft, J. A., & Cox, W. E. (2001). Investing in our future: A survey of support offered to beginning secondary science and mathematics teachers. *Science Educator, 10*(1), 1–9.

Mack, A., & Rock, I. (1998). *Inattentional blindness.* Cambridge, MA: MIT Press.

Marcus, G. (2008). *Kluge: The haphazard construction of the human mind.* New York: The Houghton Mifflin Company.

Marlow, L., Inman, D., & Betancourt-Smith, M. (1997). Beginning teachers: Are they still leaving the profession? *Clearing House, 70*(4), 211–214.

Masse, L. N. & Barnett, W. S. (2002). *A benefit cost analysis of the Abecedarian early childhood intervention.* New Brunswick, NJ: National Institute for Early Education Research. Retrieved April 19, 2008, from: http://nieer. org/resources/research/AbecedarianStudy.pdf.

Matsumura, L. C., Garnier, H., Pascal, J., & Valdes, R. (2002). Measuring instructional quality in accountability systems: Classroom assignments and student achievement. *Educational Assessment, 8*(3), 207–229.

McCaffrey, D. F., Lockwood, J. R., Koretz, D., & Hamilton, L. (2003). *Evaluating value-added models for teacher accountability.* Santa Monica, CA: Rand. Retrieved March 20, 2008, from: https://www.rand.org/pubs/monographs/2004/RAND_MG158.pdf.

McCaffrey, D. F., Lockwood, J. R., Koretz, D., Louis, T. A., & Hamilton, L. (2004). Models for value-added modeling of teacher effects. *Journal of Educational and Behavioral Statistics, 29*(1), 67–101.

Medley, D. M.,& Coker, H. (1987). The accuracy of principals' judgments of teacher performance. *Journal of Educational Research, 80*(4),242–247.

Medley, D. M., & Mitzel, H. E. (1958). A technique for measuring classroom behavior. *Journal of Educational Psychology, 49*(2), 86–92.

Medley, D. M., & Mitzel, H. E. (1963). Measuring classroom behavior by systematic observation. In N. L. Gage (Ed.), *Handbook of research on teaching* (pp. 247–328). Chicago: Rand McNally.

Merseth, K.K. (1992). First aid for first-year teachers. *Phi Delta Kappan, 73*(9), 678–683.

Meyer, R. H. (1996). Value-added indicators of school performance. In E. A. Hanushek & D. W. Jorgenson (Eds.), *Improving America's schools: The role of incentives* (pp. 197–223). Washington, DC: National Academy Press.

Milanowski, A. (2004). The relation between teacher performance evaluation scores and student achievement: Evidence from Cincinnati. *Peabody Journal of Education, 79*(4), 33–53.

Milanowski, A., & Odden, A. (2007). *A new approach to the cost of teacher turnover* (School Finance Redesign Project, Center on Reinventing Public Education, Working Paper No. 13). Seattle: University of Washington, Daniel J. Evans School of Public Affairs. Retrieved March 4, 2008, from http://www.crpe.org/cs/crpe/view/csi_pubs/172.

Miller, G.A. (1956). The magical number seven plus or minus two: Some limits on our capacity for processing information. *Psychological Review, 63*(2), 81–97.

Mishan, E.J. (1976). *Cost-benefit analysis* (2d ed.). New York: Prager.

Mitchell, K. J., Robinson, D. Z., Plake, B. S., & Knowles K. T. (Eds.). (2001). *Testing teacher candidates: The role of licensure tests in improving teacher quality.* Washington, DC: National Academy Press.

Mont, D., and Rees, D. I. (1996). The influence of classroom characteristics on high school teacher turnover. *Economic Inquiry, 34*(1), 152–167.

Moran, A., Dallat, J., & Abbott, L. (1999). Newly qualified teachers in post-primary schools in Northern Ireland: The support provided for their needs and their own vision for induction. *European Journal of Teacher Education, 22*(2), 173–189.

Moskowitz, J., & Stephens, M., (Eds.). (1997). *From students of teaching to teachers of students: Teacher induction around the Pacific Rim* (APEC Education Forum Report). Washington, DC: U.S. Department of Education for the Asian Pacific Economic Corporation. (ERIC Document Reproduction Service No. 415594).

Mosteller, F., & Moynihan, D. P. (Eds.). (1972). *On equality of educational opportunity.* New York: Random House.

Munoz, M. A., & Munoz, M. D. (2000). *Evaluating training: Return on investment and cost-benefit analysis.* (ERIC Document Reproduction Service No. ED471457).

Murnane, R. J., & Olsen, R. J. (1989). The effects of salaries and opportunity costs on duration in teaching: evidence from Michigan. *Review of Economics and Statistics, 71*(2), 347–352.

Murnane, R. J., & Olsen, R. J. (1990). The effects of salaries and opportunity costs on duration in teaching: evidence from South Carolina. *Journal of Human Resources, 25*(1), 106–124.

Murnane, R. J., & Schwinden, M. (1989). Race, gender, and opportunity: Supply and demand for new teachers in North Carolina, 1975–1985. *Educational Evaluation and Policy Analysis, 11*(2), 93–108.

Murnane, R. J., Singer, J. D., & Willett, J. B. (1988). The career paths of teachers: Implications for teacher supply and methodical lessons for research. *Educational Researcher, 17*(6), 22–30.

Murnane, R. J., Singer, J. D., Willett, J. B., Kemple, J. J., & Olsen, R. J. (1991). *Who will teach?* Cambridge, MA: Harvard University Press.

Murphy, J. (1993). What's in? What's out? American education in the nineties. *Phi Delta Kappan, 74*(8), 641–646.

Mynatt, C. R., Doherty, M. E., & Tweney, R. D. (1977). Confirmation bias in a simulated research environment: an experimental study of scientific inference. *Quarterly Journal of Experimental Psychology, 29*(1), 85–95.

National Commission on Teaching and America's Future (NCTAF). (2003). *No dream denied: A pledge to America's children.* Washington, DC: Author.

National Commission on Teaching and America's Future (NCTAF). (2005). *Induction into learning communities.* Washington, DC: Author.

Neisser, U. (1963). The multiplicity of thought. *British Journal of Psychology, 54*(1), 1–14.

Nieto, S. (Ed.). (2005). *Why we teach.* New York: Teachers College Press.

Nickerson, R. S. (1998). Confirmation bias: A ubiquitous phenomenon in many guises. *Review of General Psychology, 2*(2), 175–220.

No Child Left Behind Act of 2001 (NCLB). Pub. L. No. 107–110, 115 Stat. 1425. (2002).

Noe, R. A. (1988). An investigation of the determinants of successful assigned mentoring relationships. *Personnel Psychology, 41*(3), 457–479.

Nussbaum, M. C. (2001). The costs of tragedy: Some moral limits of cost-benefit analysis. In M. D. Adler & E.A. Posner (Eds.), *Cost-benefit analysis. Legal, economic, and philosophical perspectives* (pp. 169–200). Chicago: University of Chicago Press.

Nye, B., Konstantopoulos, S., & Hedges, L. (2004). How large are teacher effects? *Educational Evaluation and Policy Analysis, 26*(3), 237–257.

Oberski, I., Ford, K., Higgins, S., & Fisher, P. (1999). The importance of relationships in teacher education. *Journal of Education for Teaching, 25*(2), 135–150.

Odden, A., Borman, G., & Fermanich, M. (2004). Assessing teacher, classroom, and school effects, including fiscal effects. *Peabody Journal Of Education, 79*(4), 4–32.

Odell, S. J., & Ferraro, D. P. (1992). Teacher mentoring and teacher retention. *Journal of Teacher Education, 43*(3), 200–204.

Olson, L. (2000). Finding and keeping competent teachers. Quality counts 2000: Who should teach [special issue]. *Education Week, 19*(18), 12–18.

Peterson, K. D. (1987). Teacher evaluation with multiple and variable lines of evidence. *American Educational Research Journal, 24*(2), 311–317.

Peterson, K. D. (2000). *Teacher evaluation: A comprehensive guide to new directions and practices* (2nd ed.). Thousand Oaks, CA: Corwin Press.

Piaget, J. (1926). *The language and thought of the child.* London: Routledge & Kegan Paul.

Pinkovitz, W. H., Moskal, J., & Green, G. (1997). *How much does your employee turnover cost?* Madison, WI: University of Wisconsin Cooperative Extension, Center for Community Economic Development. Retrieved April 9, 2008, from http://www.uwex.edu/ces/cced/economies/turn.cfm.

Podgursky, M., Monroe, R., & Watson, D. (2004). The academic quality of public school teachers: An analysis of entry and exit behavior. *Economics of Education Review, 23*(5), 507–518.

Provasnik, S., & Dorfman, S. (2005). *Mobility in the teacher workforce: Findings from "The Condition of Education 2005"* (NCES 2005-114). Washington, DC: U.S. Department of Education, Institute of Education Sciences NCES 2005–114.

Quality counts 2003: If I can't learn from you [Special issue]. (2003, January 9). *Education Week, 22*(17). Retrieved April 1, 2008, from http://www.ed.week.org.

Quality counts 2005: No small change [Special issue]. (2005, January 6). *Education Week, 24*(17). Retrieved April 1, 2008, from http://www.ed.week.org.

Quality counts 2008: Tapping into teaching [Special issue]. (2008, January 10). *Education Week, 27*(18). Retrieved April 1, 2008, from http://www.ed.week.org.

Quartz, K. H., Thomas, A., Anderson, L., Masyn, K., Lyons, K. B. & Olsen, B. (2008). Careers in motion: A longitudinal retention study of role changing among early-career urban educators. *Teachers College Record, 110*(1), 218–250.

Raudenbush, S.W., & Bryk, A. S. (2002). *Hierarchical linear models: Applications and data analysis methods.* Thousand Oaks, CA: Sage.

Reed, D., Rueben, K. S., & Barbour, E. (2006). *Retention of new teachers in California.* San Francisco: Public Policy Institute of California.

Reynolds, A. (1992). What is competent beginning teaching? A review of the literature. *Review of Educational Research, 62*(1), 1–35.

Rice, J. K. (2003). *Teacher quality: Understanding the effectiveness of teacher attributes.* Washington, DC: Economic Policy Institute.

Riggs, L., & Scott, L. (1999, April 20). *Challenges in the retention of new teachers: The significance of structured support.* Paper presented at the annual meeting of the American Educational Research Association, Montreal, Canada.

Rivkin, S., Hanushek, E., & Kain, J. (2005). Teachers, schools, and academic achievement. *Econometrica, 73*(2), 417–458.

Robinson, P. (1981). *Perspectives on the sociology of education.* London: Routledge & Kegan Paul.

Robinson, P., & Smithers, A. (1991). *Teacher turnover* (Report to the Leverhulme Trust). Manchester, UK: University of Manchester, School of Education.

Roche, G. R. (1979). Much ado about mentors. *Harvard Business Review, 57*(1), 17–28.

Rockoff, J. E. (2008). *Does mentoring reduce turnover and improve skills of new employees? Evidence from teachers in New York City* (NBER Working Paper No. 13868). Cambridge, MA: National Bureau of Economic Research. Retrieved April 5, 2008, from http://www.nber.org/papers/w13868.

Roehrig, A. D., Bohn, C. M., Turner, J. E., & Pressley, M. (2008). Mentoring beginning primary teachers for exemplary teaching practices. *Teaching and Teacher Education, 24*(3), 684–702.

Rosenberg, M. S., Griffin, C. C., Kilgore, K. L., & Carpenter, S. L. (1997). Beginning teachers in special education: A model for providing individualized support. *Teacher Education and Special Education, 20*(4), 301–321.

Rosenholtz, S. J., & Simpson, C. (1990). Workplace conditions and the rise and fall of teachers' commitment. *Sociology of Education, 63*(4), 241–257.

Rosenshine, B. (1983). Teaching functions in instructional programs. *Elementary School Journal, 83*(4), 335–51.

Rosenshine, B., & Furst, N. (1973). The use of direct observation to study teaching. In R. M. W. Travers (Ed.), *Second handbook of research on teaching* (pp. 122–183). Chicago: Rand McNally.

Ross, J. A. (1992). Teacher efficacy and the effect of coaching on student achievement. *Canadian Journal of Education, 17*(1), 51–65.

Ross, L., Lepper, M. R., Hubbard, M. (1975). Perseverance in self-perception and social perception: biased attributional processes in the debriefing paradigm. *Journal of Personality and Social Psychology, 32*(5), 880–892.

Rothstein, J. (2007). *Do value-added models add value? Tracking, fixed effects, and causal inference* (Preliminary paper). Retrieved April 2, 2008, from: http://64.233.179.104/scholar?hl=en&lr=&q=cache:7DlojKbTqW0J:econ. lse.ac.uk/seminars/papers/labour-141207.pdf+rothstein+2007+do+value+ added+models.

Rothstein, J. (2008). *Teacher quality in educational production: Tracking, decay, and student achievement.* Retired July 1, 2008, from http://www. princeton.edu/~jrothst/workingpapers/rothstein_VAM.pdf.

Rowan, B., Correnti, R., & Miller, R. J. (2002). What large-scale, survey research tells us about teacher effects on student achievement: Insights from the prospects study of elementary schools. *Teachers College Record, 104*(8), 1525–1567.

Saldana, D. C., & Waxman, H. C. (1997). An observational study of multicultural education in urban elementary schools. *Equity and Excellence in Education, 30*(1), 40–46.

Sanders, W. (2000). Value-added assessment from student achievement data: Opportunities and hurdles. *Journal of Personnel Evaluation in Education 14*(4), 329–339.

Sanders, W. L., Ashton, J. J., & Wright, S. P. (2005, March 7). *Comparison of the effects of NBPTS certified teachers with other teachers on the rate of student academic progress.* Arlington, VA: National Board for Professional Teaching Standards. Retrieved April 5, 2008, from: http://www.nbpts.org/ UserFiles/File/SAS_final_NBPTS_report_D_-_Sanders.pdf.

Sanders, W., & Horn, B. (1998). Research findings from the Tennessee Value-Added Assessment System (TVAAS) database: Implications for educational evaluation and research. *Journal of Personnel Evaluation in Education, 12*(3), 247–256.

Sanders, W., Saxton, A., & Horn, B. (1997). The Tennessee Value-Added Assessment System: A quantitative outcomes-based approach to educational assessment. In J. Millman (Ed.), *Grading teachers, grading schools: Is student achievement a valid evaluational measure?* (pp. 137–162). Thousand Oaks, CA: Corwin Press.

Scafidi, B., Sjoquist, D. L., and Stinebrickner, T. R. (2007). Race, poverty, and teacher mobility. *Economics of Education Review, 26*(2), 145–159.

Scandura, T.A. (1992). Mentorship and career mobility: An empirical investigation. *Journal of Organizational Behavior, 13*(2), 169–174.

Scandura, T.A. & Viator, R. (1994). Mentoring in public accounting firms: An analysis of mentor-protégé relationships, mentoring functions, and protégé turnover intentions. *Accounting Organizations and Society, 19*(8), 717–734.

Schaffer, E., Stringfield, S., & Wolfe, D. (1992). An innovative beginning teacher induction program: A two-year analysis of classroom interactions. *Journal of Teacher Education, 43*(3), 181–192.

Scherer, M. (Ed.). (1999). *A better beginning: Supporting and mentoring new teachers.* Alexandria, VA: Association for Supervision and Curriculum Development.

Scherer, M. (2001). How and why standards can improve student achievement: A conversation with Robert J. Marzano. *Educational Leadership, 59*(1), 14–18.

Schochet, P. Z. (2005). *Statistical power for random assignment evaluations of education programs* (Report No. 6046-310). Washington, DC: Mathematica Policy Research, Inc. Retrieved February 5, 2008, from http://www.mathematica-mpr.com/publications/PDFs/statisticalpower.pdf.

Scott-Hendrick, L., & Childress, L. J. (2002). *The RIMS Beginning Teacher Support and Assessment Partnership: A Study of Eight Years of Collaboration.* A paper Presented at annual meeting of the American Educational Research Association Conference, New Orleans, LA.

Shen, J. (1997). Teacher retention and attrition in public schools: Evidence from SASS 91. *The Journal of Educational Research, 91*(2), 81–88.

Shen, J., & Palmer, L. B. (2005). Attrition patterns of inadequately prepared teachers. In J. R. Dangel & E. M. Guyton (Eds.), *Research on alternative and nontraditional education* (pp. 143–157). Lanham, MD: Scarecrow Education.

Shockley, R., Guglielmino, P., & Watlington, E. (2006). *The costs of teacher attrition.* Paper presented at the International Congress for School Effectiveness and Improvement, Fort Lauderdale, FL. Retrieved April 11, 2008 from: http://www.leadership.fau.edu/ICSEI2006/Papers/Shockley%20Guglielmino%20and%20Watlington.pdf.

Simon, H. (1957). *Models of man.* New York: Wiley.

Simon, A., & Boyer, E. G. (Eds.). (1974). *Mirrors for behavior III: An anthology of observation instruments.* Wyncote, PA: Communications Materials Center. (ERIC Document ED 170320)

Simons, D. J. (2000). Attentional capture and inattentional blindness. *Trends in Cognitive Sciences, 4*(4), 147–155.

Simons, D. J. & Chabris, C. F. (1999). Gorillas in our midst: sustained inattentional blindness for dynamic events. *Perception, 28*(9), 1059–1074.

Sloman, S. A. (1996). The empirical case for two systems of reasoning. *Psychological Bulletin, 119*(1), 3–22.

Slovic, P, & Fischhoff, B. (1977). On the psychology of experimental surprises. *Journal of Experimental Psychology: Human Perception and Performance, 3*(4), 544–551.

Smith, T., & Ingersoll, R. (2004). What are the effects of induction and mentoring on beginning teacher turnover? *American Educational Research Journal, 41*(3), 681–714.

Smithers, A., & Robinson, P. (2002). *Teachers leaving.* London: National Union of Teachers (NUT). Retrieved July 16, 2004, from http://www.teachers.org.uk/story.php?id=1832&startfrom=0.

Solow, R. (1981, March/April), Replies to "cost-benefit analysis: An ethical critique." *AEI Journal on Government and Society Regulation.*

Spencer, C. (2000). *1999–2000 RIMS/BTSA retention study* (Technical Report). Riverside: University of California, Graduate School of Education.

Spuhler, L., & Zetler, A. (1995). *Montana Beginning Teacher Support Program:*

Final report. Helena: Montana State Board of Education. (ERIC Document Reproduction Service No. ED390804)

Stanovich, K. E., & West, R. F. (2000). Individual differences in reasoning: Implications for the rationality debate. *Behavioral and Brain Sciences, 23*(5), 645–665.

Stempien, L. R., & Loeb, R. C. (2002). Differences in job satisfaction between general education and special education teachers. *Remedial and Special Education, 23*(5), 258–267.

Stewart, B. E. (2006). *Value-added modeling: The challenge of measuring educational outcomes.* New York: Carnegie Corporation.

Stinebrickner, T. R. (1998). An empirical investigation of teacher attrition. *Economics of Education Review, 17*(2), 127–136.

Stinebrickner, T. R. (2001). A dynamic model of teacher labor supply. *Journal of Labor Economics, 19*(1), 196–230.

Stinebrickner, T. R. (2002). An analysis of occupational change and departure from the labor force: Evidence of the reasons that teachers leave. *Journal of Human Resources, 37*(1), 192–216.

Stodolsky. S. S. (1990). Classroom observation. In J. Millman & L. Darling-Hammond (Eds.), *The new handbook of teacher evaluation: Assessing elementary and secondary school teachers* (pp. 175–190). London: Sage.

Stoel, C., & Thant, T.-S. (2002). *Teachers' professional lives: A view from nine industrialized countries.* Washington, DC: Council for Basic Education and Milken Family Foundation.

Strauss, R. P., & Sawyer, E. A. (1986). Some new evidence on teacher and student competencies. *Economics of Education Review, 5*(1), 41–48.

Strizek, G. A., Pittsonberger, J. L., Riordan, K. E., Lyter, D. M., & Orlofsky, G. F. (2006). *Characteristics of schools, districts, teachers, principals, and school libraries in the United States: 2003–04 schools and staffing survey (NCES 2006-313 Revised).* Washington: U.S. Department of Education, National Center for Education Statistics.

Strong, M., & Baron, W. (2004). An analysis of mentoring conversations with beginning teachers: Suggestions and responses. *Teaching and Teacher Education, 20*(1), 47–57.

Strong, M., & St. John, L. (2001). *A study of teacher retention: The effects of mentoring for beginning teachers* (Working Paper No. 3). Santa Cruz: University of California at Santa Cruz, New Teacher Center.

Swanson, C. B. (2003). *Who graduates? Who doesn't? A statistical portrait of public high school graduation, class of 2001.* Washington, DC: Urban Institute Education Policy Center. Retrieved March 3, 2008 from http://www.urban.org/UploadedPDF/410934_WhoGraduates.pdf.

Teddlie, C., Kirby, P. C., & Stringfield, S. (1989). Effective versus ineffective schools: Observable differences in the classroom. *American Journal of Education, 97*(3), 221–236.

Tellez, K. (1992). Mentors by choice, not design: Help-seeking by beginning teachers. *Journal of Teacher Education, 43*(3), 214–221.

Temin, P. (2002). Teacher quality and the future of America. *Eastern Economic Journal, 28*(3), 285–300.

Tepper, K., Shaffer, B. C., & Tepper, B. J. (1996). Latent structure of mentoring function scales. *Educational and Psychological Measurement, 56*(5), 848–857.

Texas Center for Educational Research (TCER). (2000). *The Cost of Teacher Turnover.* Austin, TX: Texas State Board for Educator Certification.

Theis-Sprinthall, L. (1986). A collaborative approach for mentor training: A working model. *Journal of Teacher Education, 37*(6), 13–20.

Theobald, N. D. (1990). An examination of the influence of personal, professional, and school district characteristics on public school teacher retention. *Economics of Education Review, 9*(3), 241–250.

Theobald, N. D., & Gritz, R. M. (1996). The effects of school district spending priorities on the exit paths of beginning teachers leaving the district. *Economics of Education Review, 15*(1), 11–22.

Thompson, M., Paek, P., Goe, L., & Ponte, E. (2004a). *Study of the impact of the California formative assessment and support system for teachers: Report 2. Relationship of BTSA/CFASST engagement and teacher practices* (ETS-RR-04-31). Princeton, NJ: Educational Testing Service.

Thompson, M., Paek, P., Goe, L., & Ponte, E. (2004b). *Study of the impact of the California formative assessment and support system for teachers: Report 3. Relationship of BTSA/CFASST engagement and student achievement* (ETS-RR-04-32). Princeton, NJ: Educational Testing Service.

Thompson, M., Paek, P., Goe, L., & Ponte, E. (2004c). *Study of the impact of the California formative assessment and support system for teachers: Research summary.* Princeton, NJ: Educational Testing Service.

Tickle, L. (2000). Teacher probation resurrected: England 1999–2000. *Journal of Education Policy, 15*(6), 701–713.

Townsend, D. R. (1976). Bilingual interaction analysis: The development and status. In A. Simoes, Jr. (Ed.), *The bilingual child.* New York: Academic Press.

U.S. Census Bureau. (2005). *Current population survey (CPS), October Supplement, 1972 and 2005.* Washington, DC: Author.

U.S. Department of Education, National Center for Education Statistics. (2005). *The Condition of Education 2005* (NCES 2005-094). Washington, DC: Author.

Veenman, S., & Denessen, E. (2001). The coaching of teachers: Results of five training studies. *Educational Research and Evaluation,7*(4), 385 – 417.

Villani, S. (2002). *Mentoring programs for new teachers: Models of induction and support.* Thousand Oaks, CA: Corwin Press.

Villar, A., & Strong, M. (2007). Is mentoring worth the money? A benefit-cost analysis and five-year rate of return of a comprehensive mentoring program for beginning teachers. *ERS Spectrum, 25*(3), 1–17.

Vygotsky, L. S. (1987). Thinking and speech. In R. W. Rieber & A. S. Carton (Eds.), *The collected works of L. S. Vygotsky: Vol. 1. Problems of general psychology.* New York: Plenum Press. (Original work published 1934)

Wang, J., & Odell, S. J. (2007). An alternative conception of mentor–novice relationships: Learning to teach in reform-minded ways as a context. *Teaching and Teacher Education, 23*(4), 473–489.

Wang, J., Odell, S.J., & Schwille, S.A. (2008). Effects of teacher induction on beginning teachers' teaching: A critical review of the literature. *Journal of Teacher Education, 59*(2), 132–152.

Wang, J., Strong, M., & Odell, S. J. (2004). Mentor–novice conversations about teaching: A comparison of two U.S. and two Chinese cases. *Teachers College Record, 106*(4), 775–813.

Wason, P. C. (1960). On the failure to eliminate hypotheses in a conceptual task. *Quarterly Journal of Experimental Psychology, 12,* 129–140.

Wason, P. C. (1971). Problem solving and reasoning. *British Medical Bulletin, 27*(3), 206–210.

Wason, P. C., & Johnson-Laird, P. N. (Eds.). (1968). *Thinking and reasoning.* Baltimore: Penguin.

Webster, W., & Mendro, R. (1997). The Dallas Value-Added Accountability System. In J. Millman (Ed.), *Grading teachers, grading schools: Is student achievement a valid evaluational measure?* (pp. 81–99). Thousand Oaks, CA: Corwin Press.

Weiss, E. (1999). Perceived workplace conditions and first-year teachers' morale, career choice, commitment, and planned retention: A secondary analysis. *Teaching and Teacher Education, 15*(8), 861–880.

Whalen, T., & Wright, D. (1999). Methodology for cost-benefit analysis of web-based tele-learning: Case study of the Bell Online Institute. *American Journal of Distance Education, 13*(1), 25–43.

Wisniewski, L., & Gargiulo, R. M. (1997). Occupational stress and burnout among special educators: A review of the literature. *Journal of Special Education, 31*(3), 325–346.

Wollman-Bonilla, J. E. (1997). Mentoring as a two-way street. *Journal of Staff Development, 18*(3), 50–52.

Wong, H. K. (2004). Induction programs that keep new teachers teaching and improving. *NASSP Bulletin, 88*(638), 41–58.

Wong, H. K., Britton, T., & Ganser, T. (2005). What the world can teach us about new teacher induction. *Phi Delta Kappan, 86*(5), 379–384.

Wright, P., Horn, S., & Sanders, W. (1997). Teachers and classroom heterogeneity: Their effects on educational outcomes. *Journal of Personnel Evaluation in Education 11*(1), 57–67.

Youngs, P. A. (2002). *State and district policy related to mentoring and new teacher induction in Connecticut.* New York: National Commission on Teaching and America's Future.

Yusko, B., & Feiman-Nemser, S. (2008). Embracing contraries: Combining assistance and assessment in new teacher induction. *Teachers College Record, 110*(5), 923–953.

Zabel, R. H., & Zabel, M. K. (2001). Revisiting burnout among special education teachers: Do age, experience, and preparation still matter? *Teacher Education and Special Education, 24*(2), 128–139.

Zey, Michael G. (1984). *The mentor connection.* Homewood, IL: Dow Jones-Irwin.

Index

About the Author

Michael Strong has been the Director of Research at the University of California's New Teacher Center in Santa Cruz since it was founded in 1998. He has a master's degree in applied linguistics from the University of London and a doctorate in education specializing in language and reading development, from the University of California at Berkeley. Before coming to the New Teacher Center he was Director of Research at the Langley Porter Psychiatric Institute's Center on Deafness at the University of California at San Francisco, where he pioneered the use of a bilingual approach to educate deaf children.